Topaz Publishing

READING ENTERTAINMENT FOR THE ENTIRE FAMILY

Copyright© January 2012, Beth Wedding

Cover Art: Dawne Dominque Copyright January 2012

Editor: Kase J. Reed

Line Editor: Topaz Publishing

Genre: Topaz Whisper, Contemporary Romance

ISBN: TPEB000000017

ISBN-13: 978-0615594422
ISBN-10: 0615594425

Topaz Publishing, LLC USA

Topaz Publishing, LLC

Dirty Lace

Misfits, least likely to succeed

Seven poverty-stricken misfits form a common bond through a high school dance line. Ten years later, a small town parade unites these women for a startling reunion. Though successful in life, each one has tasted the joy or defeat of true romance. Sworn blood sisters for life, these friends discover that a snotty young heiress had planted her deceitful roots among them. Had their friendship and sacrifices meant nothing to Lace? Contemporary, Sweet, & Christian Romance Beth Wedding

Available in E-Book, Kindle, and Print

Thank you for buying a product of Topaz Publishing

Quality Reading for the Entire Family

Dirty Lace

By

Beth Wedding

CHAPTER ONE

Timothy had a refined voice, though raspy with age. "Give it to me," he demanded. With a desperate lunge, he tried to grasp the smoldering cigarette clenched between Lace's lips. "Take that infernal thing out of your mouth, Young Lady!"

With her height of six feet, Lace slipped her willowy body from Timothy's limited reach. Her slow halting voice elevated sharply, "Stop that. This is my kitchen and I'll smoke wherever I please." She placed the cigarette in an ashtray then carefully peeled back the foil on an aluminum container. Closing her green eyes, she inhaled the moist hickory-smoked aroma of BBQ ribs. "That smells divine."

"And how would you know?" Timothy asked, leaning his robust frame against the kitchen counter. "The only smoke you enjoy is that horrible smell in your hair and on your clothes."

Lace dipped her finger into the sauce, then licked the tasty remains. "There is nothing wrong with my taste buds." She turned her gaze toward Timothy. "You really seem nervous about this class reunion. It's not like you have anything to hide." She smoothed her short skirt, sat down, then perched her freshly shaven legs upon the barstool beside her.

Timothy closed his eyes in frustration. "Why shouldn't I be nervous? You led this entire town to believe I was your father. Furthermore, what was wrong with admitting *you* were the heiress of a multimillion dollar industry?" He threw his palms upward in dismay. "And, just look at you! I've tried to make a lady out of you. Where did I fail?" He folded his arms and shook his head.

Lace thumped ashes into the ashtray. "You know how people are. At the time, I just wanted to fit in. Besides, there's nothing wrong with me. I'm just my own person."

Timothy sighed, and ran his fingers through his silver curls. "Ahh Lace, you've lived a lie for so many years. You just didn't turn out the way your parents would have expected."

Lace's emerald eyes sparked with interest then narrowed at the mere mention of her deceased parents. "Don't bring my parents into this, Timothy. You did a damn good job of raising me!"

"See, that's what I mean." Timothy cringed. "Just listen to yourself! Your parents would not have approved of such language. Please restrain from using profanity and all other sorts of vulgarity …at least, while your guests are here. What are your friends going to think of you, after all these years?"

She lit another cigarette, and blew smoke in Timothy's face. Her deep voice lingered over her sarcasm. "Look, you can stop pretending to be my father. I smoked in high school, and I used a few flavorful words. Why should I change now?"

Fanning the smoke, Timothy sputtered, "You should have a refined quality like your Christian mother, God rest her soul. Instead, you are discourteous, insensitive, sarcastic, and spiteful. I'm surprised you had any friends at all, Lace Garnett." Timothy marched toward the sink to wash his smoke tainted hands.

This time, Lace blew her smoke upward. "Timothy, people loathe me because I'm honest. And, I am who I am."

With water running Timothy admitted, "Well Miss Honesty, a ten year reunion is a fine time to come out of the closet—an heiress, indeed!"

Annoyed by his distressing behavior, Lace crushed her cigarette in the ashtray then stood up. Nonchalantly, she strolled toward him. She towered above his thinning crown, trapping him against the sink.

He swept his eyes past Lace's cleavage, and then looked into her eyes. "Ghastly."

"Who am I hiding from now?" Lace pressed.

Turning with force, Timothy snatched a paper towel, and crushed it in his hand. He locked eyes with hers, and ran his fingers over the manicured hairs of his white beard. "Don't try to intimidate me, young lady. I knew you in your mother's womb."

Lace touched his chest with a sharp finger. "I said. Who am I hiding from now? Soon, my friends will discover I'm a spoiled heiress who doesn't give a sh… "

"Lace!" Timothy interrupted. He grasped the sharp finger imbedded in his chest.

"…darn what people think of me," she continued, with her body defensive and stiff.

Accustomed to Lace's vile demeanor, Timothy kept his temper. He eased from the mousetrap she had fashioned for him. "It isn't about what people think, Lace." Timothy turned to face the doorway. He gazed around the room, and stretched out his arms to encompass the modernized kitchen. "This is your inheritance. Just look at what you own. Gaze across that exquisite courtyard. You own all of this—a home in California, and an enormous lodge in Denver. You owe your comfortable life to your parents. Sayers Electronics has a reputation to uphold.

Now, for the sake of your saintly father, and the company's name, please use restraints while your guests are here. You represent Sayers Electronics now! I don't care what the media says; this is no way for an heiress to behave." His shoulders slumped as he sauntered to the walk-in refrigerator.

Timothy peered over his shoulder.

Lace looked at her watch. She sighed and propped herself back on her stool.

In a softer tone, he admitted, "I've been a father figure to you all your life. I promised your father I would take care of you. It was your idea to pose as my daughter."

As if assaulted, Lace placed two fingers on her forehead. The large diamond on her ring finger reflected the midday light. She whispered,

"Not again." Lace peered through her slender fingers and moaned. "Why-must-you-constantly-bring this up?" She massaged her temples. "You didn't have to play along with my plan."

Timothy narrowed his eyes, his voice now rife with frustration. "Yes," he admitted, gnashing his teeth. "I could have said no! But, for the love of all that is Holy, I never understood why you didn't want anyone to know *who* you are." He bent to ramble through the lower shelves of the walk-in. With lemons clenched in his fingers, he walked back to the door, and threw Lace a disappointed glance. "You look so much like your mother. It's difficult *not* to cater to you." He shook his head. "You went to a public school, for Pete's sake. You bought your clothing from local merchants. Most of your clothing was not name brand. After one washing, they faded or lost their shape."

He turned his attention back to his task, and pulled a large relish tray from the walk-in. "Sweetheart, it is beyond me why you wanted to live like a pauper. You could have attended the best Universities; mingled with people of status—but you wanted to attend a local University."

Placing the cold tray on the counter, Timothy continued, "Now, the truth is catching up with you. I tried to warn you of future consequences. You intentionally deceived an entire town."

Lace covered her ears as if frustration was eating her alive. "Must we discuss this today, Timothy?" Again, she looked at her watch. "It's almost one o'clock, my guests will arrive soon."

"It isn't that easy, Lace. I've been a key character in this *nest* of humiliation for many years." Timothy rearranged the relish tray and persisted with his conversation. "You owe me the compensation of discussing it now."

In her heart, Lace knew he wanted his last performance to come soon. His life had also been a lie.

He turned his attention back to the tray and scoffed. "I want to know if you achieved your desired outcome, my dear." Timothy grew silent for a moment. "Or, was it all for nothing? Just think — a limo could have picked you up from school each day. Instead, you insisted I drive you to school in a common, mid-sized economy car

My God! You and your friends were caught stealing food from the school cafeteria.

You infiltrated the homes of your friends and led them to believe you were just like them. You were branded a juvenile delinquent for stealing only God knows what. Drugs. Alcohol. Boys. Men. The list is as long as my arm. What were you trying to prove?" Timothy's brows furrowed, revealing years of worry.

Lace's lean frame seemed to shrink beneath his reproachful words. On a whimper she pleaded, "Are you finished? Please tell me you're finished."

He ignored her appeal, swiped a tempting carrot stick, then proceeded with his tirade. "Oh no, I'm not quite finished with you." He shook the carrot in her face. "You made my life unbearable. You wanted people to believe you lived in the servant's quarters with me. You acted as if you were contented in my small, two-bedroom cottage; only to scamper up the walkway when your friends left, and steal away to the luxurious comforts of your own room. You told people your mother, or my pretend wife, was dead. What a ridiculous charade, Lace Garnett!"

He paused for a moment. "This is utterly ridiculous. You, Madam, employ me — your father's faithful valet." His cheeks reddened.

"Under your sober request, I enrolled you in public school, and pretended to be your guardian. Because this town was your parents hide-away, these people had no idea they owned *Sayers Electronics*." He popped the carrot into his mouth and chewed. "Now, ten years have passed. The game is over." He shook his head, and added, "What are your dance line buddies going to think of your deceitful behavior, now?"

The doorbell rang. Timothy looked toward the door, and pulled his collar straight. After hoisting his dark-blue trousers, he groomed himself and took one last shot at Lace. "If you had accepted the fact that you owned a multimillion dollar industry, you would have nothing to explain. Spoiled. Indeed!" After having his say, he walked toward the foyer.

CHAPTER TWO

Lace looked toward the foyer as Timothy disappeared from sight and grimaced. It seemed Timothy took every opportunity to rub her nose in the fact that she wanted to be just like everyone else. During that time, she was a lost teenager who only wanted to fit in. A tired nervousness crept over her body. After years of intense lies, she *was* ready to confess. She didn't care what anyone thought—or did she? With anxious fingers, Lace fanned her blonde locks about her shoulders, stood and brushed ashes from her skirt, boosted her bra, then perked her lips to freshen her gloss.

Ten years had passed. It had been her idea to fly-in her old friends for the reunion. After all, everyone needed to pitch-in to make the float for Saturdays' parade. Admitting she was wealthy was the least of her worries. These women were her friends—real friends. They didn't love her for what she had; they loved her for who she was. In that area, her plan had worked.

After ten years, what would they all look like? Yes, she had gained a few adult pounds, enhanced her lips, cheated father time out of sagging boobs and had a few other procedures done, but she had no idea what to expect from them.

With sandal-clad feet, Lace walked briskly down the hall toward the game room. Inhaling, she pressed her fingers to her quivering stomach. An elegant hallway mirror caught her reflection and displayed her beauty. The skin around her eyes was smooth, complemented by an arched, freshly tweezed brow. Her skin was still firm. She pressed her plump lips together and noted how sensual they appeared.

Because she used the newest tanning techniques at 'BLAZE's Salon' her skin was healthy and moist. Turning to admire her tight rear, she stifled a loud, "Yes!", and winked at herself. Her trainer had worked a small miracle. She still had it. Who said she was vain? Well, perhaps just a little.

In an effort to tidy the large game room, Lace cast her gaze about the spacious area.

Dirty Lace

Although Anna, her maid, had gone to New Mexico to visit her parents, she'd left the mansion clean and in order. Elevating her eyes toward the vaulted ceiling, she noticed the fans were off. As she touched the panel against the wall, Lace looked out the patio door. The well-designed pool area had cost a small fortune. No doubt, they'd spend a great deal of time there.

The distant sound of teens during horseplay echoed in her ears; a memory she had long since pushed aside. Though considered a misfit, her teen years had been the best years of her life. With face aglow, Lace recalled swimming in an overpopulated, and filthy, public pool. Brooklyn was a poor swimmer, and Lace often took advantage of that fact. At that time, all Brooklyn wanted was a pool of her own. The crowded pool drove her mad. It broke her heart to deceive Brooklyn. She loved all her friends. However, Brooklyn was closer to her than the others. They all took an oath before graduation. As blood sisters, they vowed to keep in touch. Sadly, she had only kept in touch with Brooklyn.

Lace had sworn that today, she would answer all their questions, and of course, they would answer hers. Would they still feel the same about her? At that time, being loved for an enormous heart was better than being loved for a large bank account. She had faked her entire lifestyle just to fit in. A blast of feminine laughter broke her concentration. Lace turned just as Timothy darkened the doorway.

Timothy ushered an excited female into the game room. "Ms. Brooklyn Beset," he announced formally.

A squeal pierced the air. Beside him, a slender woman with bobbed hair leaped forward to hug her friend. Her almond shaped eyes displayed the color of rich brown cocoa. They widened with anticipation. "Lace! How in the world have you been, Captain?"

"Not me, but you, First Lieutenant. How are the wedding plans coming along?"

Brooklyn drew in an excited breath. "Great. Winston is fantastic. I'm glad you made me go to that football game with you. This time, you did good."

"I'm always good. I see you finally found a hairstyle that flatters your face. I've always loved your hair," she said, fingering the silky, jet-black locks.

"You still live in the cottage across the way?"

Lace pursed her lips and frowned. "Well."

Before Lace could answer, Brooklyn continued her questions. "Are they letting us rent this place for our reunion? I've always admired this house. Simply breathtaking." Brooklyn parted her lips in awe as she took in her regal surroundings.

"I'll tell you all about it. Later," Lace added, pushing Brooklyn toward the sofa.

Brooklyn turned to look over her shoulder. "This place must have cost a fortune to rent. I always thought it was a museum or something. Does Timothy still work here?"

"Ahh. I'll tell you about that too. It's really a cute story," Lace managed, stroking her friend's back. Their voices trailed off into the depths of the game room.

The doorbell rang again, and like a dutiful servant, Timothy attended the door. Shortly afterwards, he stood in the doorway of the game room, a vinyl garment bag draped across his arm. When he was able to get Lace's attention, he announced, "Third Line Lieutenant. Mrs. Shelda Jackson."

Shelda pushed her way around Timothy. Her spiraled reddish-brown curls were pulled into a thick bushy ponytail. With her hands, mimicking a megaphone, she shook her hips and recited an old dance line chant. "Cougars are the…"

Lace and Brooklyn clapped their hands to keep time. "Best!" they chanted.

"Greater than the…" Shelda yelled.

"Rest!"

"Tigers, you'd better run!" Shelda blasted.

"Cause Cougars are number one! Seniors 2002, Rule! Go Cougars!"

They all leaped into the air, laughing. "Go Cougars!"

Lace coughed and held her chest. "I should have known you would try that old dance line crap. How have you been?" she asked, hugging the slightly overweight woman. "How are the kids, Zoey and Patricia?"

"Lace. That's Joey and Melissa. You are so bad with names. Those aren't even my kids. My daughter is Katelyn. Katelyn. I only have one. You're trying to give me Brooklyn's kids. You're terrible."

Lace grinned. "I am not. I just love those little crumb snatchers. To show my devotion—one day I'll buy an orphanage and burn it down," she kidded. "Putting on a few pounds, huh?"

"You can tell?" Shelda frowned. "I had hoped no one would notice." She hung her head in remorse, her hazel eyes seemed to search the floor.

Lace inflated her cheeks like a chipmunk, and crossed her eyes. "No. I couldn't tell at all."

"Stop that silly." She shoved Lace playfully. "So, I've put on a few pounds. You can't imagine what I've lost over the past few months to get ready for this reunion."

"Sweetie, you would not have survived the cut for Friday's field performance. Mother Cougar wouldn't let cows on the football field." She hugged her again.

Shelda whistled as she took in her elegant surroundings. "You rented this place—just for us? You must have fallen into a heap of money. I always wondered what this place looked like on the inside...pulled a few strings, huh?"

Lace's nervous laughter echoed through the game room. "Yes and no. Come on. I'll tell you all about it, later. Timothy will get the rest of your things."

Pointing toward the door with her thumb, Shelda whispered, "I saw Olivia driving up in her new sports car. Guess she didn't want to fly." Pretending to cast a fishing rod, Shelda snickered. "I heard she snagged a lawyer." She reeled in the make-believe line. "He broke the line getting away."

Lace sneered then folded her arms. "He left Olivia? Nah! I don't believe it. She doesn't have any trouble snagging a man. She probably kicked *him* out of her life. You know Olivia, she's fussy about her men. That crazy woman will throw away a perfectly good man in a heartbeat." Lace lovingly stroked Shelda's hair. Come on in, sweetie. We've got a diet to ruin."

Brooklyn rushed toward Shelda with her arms outstretched. "Not before I get my hug!" She threw her arms around Shelda. "How are you?" she asked, scanning Shelda from head to toe.

Shelda nodded and patted her flabby tummy. "I'm good. How have you been since the funeral?"

Squinting painfully, Brooklyn admitted, "Well, you know, losing a husband is hard. Wayne was my life. I still get a little misty, even with a new guy in my life." Her voice grew lively. "Yep. I've met Mr. Almost Right!"

"I'm happy for you." Shelda smiled. "You deserve it. I've got to bring you up to date on my latest happenings. It's like reading a page from a cheap tabloid." She removed her hair band. A mass of shimmering spirals settled about her shoulders.

Once again, Timothy entered the room. The women looked toward the door in anticipation. "Lieutenant, Olivia Talbert."

Olivia's exotic dark eyes narrowed into glints of excitement at the sight of her old sisterhood. She pushed Timothy absently to the side, her raven braids swinging wildly in the air. Snapping her fingers, she wriggled in a seductive manor. Her full lips spouted, "Cougars are the…"

The three chanted, "Best!"

"Greater than the…"

"Rest! Okay — okay," Lace declared. "That's enough. I'm not going to be chanting that bull crap all night."

"Fun Sucker!" they said, giggling and hugging each other.

Brooklyn stopped grinning and took interest in a large painting on the wall. It was a lonesome picture of a bayou in Louisiana. She studied the painting intensely, stroking the canvas. "I really like this painting, Lace. Help me find one just like it."

"I will if you don't spaz on me." Lace slipped between her and the painting. "Why are you rubbing that painting?"

Brooklyn smiled softly, cast her gaze toward the floor, then quietly walked away.

Concerned, Lace tilted her head. "What's that all about?" She wondered aloud.

As the girls helped themselves to refreshments, tight shoes came off tired feet, and cold drinks were poured. Olivia gazed around the room. "Girl, this place is bling city. Did you marry-up with the old geezer who owned this place? I'll bet he has one foot in the grave." As she peered out the window, she fawned over the immaculate lawn. "Girl. I'll help you put him out of his misery."

Lace shuddered. "Such language, and from a lawyer!"

Olivia looked up the stairs. "First, I'm human, and then I'm a lawyer." She walked toward the patio door to admire the enclosed pool area. "Hey! I figured if you offered to pay for our flights, you must be wiping your royal butt with large bills."

Dirty Lace

As Lace carried a small cheese tray over to Shelda, a guilty smiled tugged at her lips. "That's a long story, Olivia."

While Lace was in route, Olivia reached for a strawberry. "Somehow, I always felt you'd land a millionaire."

Lace jerked her head in Olivia's direction. "And why would you think that?" She stared at Timothy, who smirked and walked away.

Olivia bit into the juicy strawberry and smiled. "Girl. Your Mae West attitude was a dead give-away. Now, tell us all about him and don't hold back on the juicy stuff either."

CHAPTER THREE

Lace was relieved when the doorbell rang. Timothy broke the urgency of the conversation. "I'll get the door." His steel-gray eyes cast an, *I told you so,* as he strutted past her.

"Oh shut up," Lace whispered under her breath.

Timothy returned shortly. Behind him, large green eyes peered from sun-deprived skin. A head thick with short red hair bobbed with excitement. In her tiny voice, she squeaked, "Cougars are the…" she stretched to see over Timothy's shoulder.

Timothy stopped her cold. "They've finished with that part of their visit, Miss. Dobson."

"Oh." She smiled, then covered her mouth. "I'm sorry," she said, in a soft breathy tone. "I'm just so excited."

"Allow me to assist you with your luggage." Timothy reached for Yara's bags. She darted ahead of him, carrying her laptop.

"Hey guys."

A pack of squealing females responded. "Yara!" They all started for the redhead at once. Snuggling, they encased her petite frame in a group hug.

Lace observed Yara's hair. "Second Lieutenant. You've cut your hair. I thought you'd never cut that greasy mess." She fingered Yara's short red hair. "No human being needed that much hair. It was draining your ability to think rationally." She looked downward and winked. "Boob job, right?"

Yara blushed. "Credit card, same as cash."

"You look awesome, Shortcake." Lace gushed. "Now, get out of my face, you're ruining *my* moment. How do you keep that tiny figure?"

Yara stroked her stomach and stated proudly, "I just exercise, eat right, and drink plenty of water." She placed her laptop on the sofa.

Looking Yara up and down, Lace shook her head in disbelief. "Eat right, exercise? That's just bull sh-."

"Lace!" Timothy barked.

Rolling her green eyes toward the ceiling, Lace changed her statement. "I mean, I do all those things and I still look like hell."

Timothy snapped his jowls impatiently. "She's a lost cause," he mumbled.

Shelda picked up a rare vase. "Where is that cute hunka meat you call a half-brother?"

From the foyer Lace called, "You've never met him, huh? He's in Miami. …has his own business now."

Shelda licked her pouty lips. "I should have married him. He was just too foxy to roam without a leash."

"Well, now he has baby flab around the middle. He was foxy, now that hunka meat is just a fat…" Remembering Timothy's warning, she stopped.

The girls settled in. They scattered themselves over the sofa as they talked and caught up on the latest gossip. Seated on the floor, Brooklyn asked, "Has anyone heard from Tessa or Satin?"

Olivia spoke up. "Satin? Oh, you mean Scraps. She said she'd be here. Tessa moved to Detroit. I work with that skank." She closed her eyes tightly and wrenched her neck in disapproval. "You would *not* believe who she wants her new conquest to be." Without giving anyone a chance to answer, she closed her statement. "My boss!"

Brooklyn frowned. "Shut up! Tessa. Law school. I thought she'd make her living as a prostitute. …just loved hopping in and out of strange beds."

Shelda sipped her tea. "I know, right? Did she taste your man too?" Sticking her finger inside her glass, she stirred her drink.

Yara smiled. "I'd better keep my Houston away from her."

Olivia pulled her braids into a ponytail and secured them. "Well, she has the hots for my boss. This makes my life miserable because she's always around. She feels that if she gets me fired, she can just move in on the firm and take my place."

Lace picked up a lipstick-soiled napkin and tossed it into the trash. "Now, that is one child who's in denial. I think her brain is stuffed with whatever she has in her breasts."

"Some of that junk is bad for your health," Yara informed, "I've got the new stuff in these jewels." She hoisted her ample bust.

Olivia frowned. "Yara, your jugs were already huge. Why the implants?"

"I know they were. I was scared they'd get flabby because they *were* so large."

Lace teased as she lowered herself into an EZ chair. "Talk about headlights. Honk-honk! Speaking of honkers, Kayleigh called. ...said she couldn't make it. ...something about having to work."

"That's too bad," Olivia acknowledged. "I heard she kinda fell on hard times. Three kids. The youngest has Autism."

Yara widened her eyes. "Wow! You never know what your future holds. Kayleigh was voted most likely to succeed."

Shelda agreed, "O. M. G. She was smart as a whip. I heard she still lives here in Cougar County."

Brooklyn crooned, "That's punishment in itself. Everyone should have the opportunity to pull themselves up."

"Well, she shouldn't have gotten pregnant before graduation." Lace snorted.

"Lace," Yara scolded. "That's so mean. We all make mistakes. She married Buck. It just didn't work out. I heard he was drinking and abusing her."

"Shut up!" Shelda gasped. "She's too sweet for that kind of life."

"It happens every day." Yara stroked her arm as if she were cold. "I'm going to miss seeing her. She was so funny. Let's give her a call before we leave, okay?"

"Great idea." Brooklyn nodded. "We could all have lunch together like old times."

Appearing anxious, Shelda parted her lips. "Lace Garnett! I don't know about the rest of these guys, but I always knew you'd make it big." She looked at the women seated around her. "Guys. Didn't you think that out of all of us, Lace would be the one to become successful?"

Brooklyn took a sip and sat her cup aside. "I sorta had a feeling she was something special."

Olivia spoke up. "Me too! Girl, I could tell by the swing in your hips that you had it going-on. The guys knew it, too."

Catching her breath, Lace reddened. "Oh, you guys. I'll explain all of this, soon. It's a really, funny story. You guys will have a good laugh."

Yara took a small sip from her fruit punch. "Your dad is so helpful. He still looks the same."

"Ah, my dad — yeah, well. Timothy — Ah." Lace paused and scratched her head. "That's part of my surprise."

"Well. When are you going to tell us this great news?" Brooklyn snuggled herself deep into the plush sofa.

"Soon." Lace averted her eyes. Clapping her hands, she called everyone's attention. "Ladies, ladies. I would like to thank all of you for coming to the Cougar Charms Dance Line Reunion. As you know, we have gathered to make plans for the Annual Cougar County Parade. We are responsible for the Cougar Charms float."

The doorbell rang. Timothy stood up. "One moment, please. Miss Satin's flight was delayed. Perhaps, she's here."

Lace continued to talk as Timothy stepped behind her. "The parade is Saturday, at two o'clock. Our dance line will feature a float in the Cougar County's Holiday Parade. The chamber of commerce has requested that our school present floats from various clubs and organizations.

Of course, our class will be featured this year. So. We have work to do — I want to hear rich ideas about floats. I did pay your airfares, so

I know you are all officially cheap skates. But, I love each and every one of you."

"She must mean it" Shelda announced, while nodding. "You know Lace doesn't say anything she doesn't mean."

Yara rolled her eyes. "I know, right."

Lace went on with her speech. "I want you to know that everyone will be staying here for the duration of the weekend. During this time, there will be no men allowed, except in my room." The girls giggled. "And, we will be eating BBQ for dinner." She extended her arms toward the ceiling and waited. "What? No applause." Puzzled, the girls simply looked at each other. "Did I mention the fact that the food is being catered by Everitt's BBQ?"

A cheer went up. Brooklyn sighed. "Everitt's. There goes my diet. I haven't had good BBQ in years."

CHAPTER FOUR

Lace noticed that Timothy's footsteps seemed delayed as he walked down the hallway. Although she heard two voices there was a familiar concern in Timothy's voice. She knew that tone all too well, and it troubled her. Her worry transferred to each of the others in turn. With bewildered expressions, they searched each other's eyes. An eerie silence fell upon the room. Timothy's large frame filled the doorway.

Yara held her hand loosely over her mouth. "Something is wrong, guys. I hope nothing has happened to Scraps."

Each of them stood. After all this time, was Satin still one of them? Under pressure, her parents moved away. Satin, once a rebellious teen, had damaged her family's name and reputation. However, the girls still loved her. After all, they were sworn blood sisters.

Timothy stepped aside and unveiled a very pregnant Satin. "Eeek!" they squealed.

"Scraps!" Shelda rushed toward her with extended arms. She placed her palms on Scraps stomach. "May I?"

Satin was silent. She gazed at Shelda with sarcastic disgust. "Why of course."

The girls fondled her, asking her questions all at once. Olivia went first. "Girl. What happened to you? One day you were here, then the next day you were gone."

Lace's rich voice sliced through the crowd. "Will someone please let her sit down?"

Yara ran to the sofa and moved a pillow. Patting the sofa, she instructed, "Sit here."

While the girls ushered Satin to the sofa, Lace scolded her. "You should *not* have come. We didn't know you were about to push out a rug rat!"

"Guys," she fussed, sweeping her blonde hair behind her ear. "Stop it. I'm okay. I wanted to come. Besides, the baby isn't due for another month."

"Oh." They each gave a sigh of relief.

Yara's voice started to crack, "What happened to you, Scraps?"

"Scraps." Satin laughed. "I haven't heard that name in years." She fixed the pillow behind her back. "I prefer, Satin. I'm all grown up now. I'm just plain old, Satin."

Shelda pushed past the others. "Here's some punch. After you rest, you can tell us what happened. Why did you leave?"

"That's her personal business." Lace narrowed her eyes.

"Come on guys," Satin cajoled. "I don't mind telling. After all, we are still friends, right?" She patted Olivia's hand, which was resting on her shoulder. "Good friends."

Lace would not let it rest. "You don't need to tell these knuckleheads anything!"

"Lace." She raised her hand to halt Lace's conversation. "I want to talk. After all, the internet was not good enough for Lace. She hired a private investigator to find me."

Olivia shrieked, "Shut- up!" She turned to face Lace, who was pacing beside her. "You hired an investigator?"

"Guys. I... I..." Lace stammered.

"Never mind," Satin ordered calmly. "I'm here now, and I want to talk. Now, sit down and listen."

Satin made eye contact with the curious women. "When, I got into trouble with the kids—the ones my dad called, The Cult. Things changed for me. See, we weren't a cult at all. We just wore black, pierced our brows, slept in the cemetery, and refused to eat meat. To our parents, this was a cult. Anyways, after Lady Sorrels came up dead, my folks thought we had something to do with it. They took me away in the middle of the night."

Olivia picked up her drink. "What really happened to Lady Sorrels?"

Satin shrugged. "Some believed she was stabbed to death. But I know what actually happened that night."

Olivia winced. "Get out. I heard you guys sacrificed her or something."

"Yeah, I heard that, too." Satin scratched her tight belly. "Guys, I swear this is the truth. On that night, we were doing our usual thing in the cemetery. You know, smoking weed, doing a little drinking. It was me, Tang, Gypsy, and Shick. Suddenly, we heard this truck driving into the cemetery's gate. From where we were standing, we could tell it was an old Ford with rusted doors. The side panel was spray painted with primer. There was a man driving the vehicle. He looked to be about forty or so.

The man's face was hideous, and contorted with anguish. That appearance is etched into my mind. Sometimes, I still have nightmares." She touched her own hair. "Dark hair lay flat to his square head. It appeared to be wet.

While an eerie damp mist fell over the cemetery, Gypsy, being the chicken that she is, whimpered. Although the man was getting out of the truck, you could tell he'd heard her. He jerked his head upwards and listened. Then, he turned his head as if searching for the source. Sunken eyes scanned the wooded area beyond the graves.

By the moonlight, we could see the man was wearing a bloody, plaid, black and white shirt. He was medium built, and gaunt. Plus, he was sweating like a racehorse. We made Gypsy get quiet. Because he went back to his work, we were sure he didn't know we were there.

Then, we saw him opening his tailgate. He pulled a heavy trash bag off the back of the truck. It hit the ground with a kinda squishing sound. Whatever he had inside, had to be watery. We thought it was trash or a dead animal at first. But Tang, our leader, suggested otherwise. We crouched behind the mausoleum, watching and listening.

The jerk took a shovel from the back of the truck, then he gave the bag a few strong whacks. "Look what you made me do!" he yelled.

Simultaneously, Gypsy let out a stream of nervous pee. The warm urine hit the fall air and created a steamy appearance around her thighs. That was a dead giveaway. If that monster had looked up, he would have seen the vapor coming from behind the mausoleum. I took off my jacket and covered her legs.

I don't know why she even joined our gang. Weiner. She was huffing and puffing as if she was having an asthma attack. I just knew he'd hear us. At the time, I was wearing fingerless leather gloves. I grabbed her face and stuffed my hand over her mouth. We were all terrified that this bimbo was going to give us away.

When we heard digging sounds, Tang looked at me and placed his finger to his lips. He peeked from hiding once more. I knew the man was trying to bury the bag. Funny thing—we knew every inch of that cemetery. He dug a grave for Lady Sorrels right beside her deceased husband. That's where he dumped the bloody trash bags. He dug and cursed, saying nonsense things like, "I told you I loved you. Why didn't you love me back?"

Then, he stopped digging for a while, sat down, and drank from a flat bottle. Of course, we knew better than to be seen. I know he dumped Lady in our cemetery, but I assure you, none of us killed her. Her body was dismembered by that jerk in the Ford truck. It's been ten years. The police should have found him by now." She chuckled and rested her hand atop her large belly.

Olivia gnashed her teeth. "God woman! Why didn't you guys report this joker? He's still out there someplace."

Satin turned to face her. "Are you freaking kidding me? I'm not messing with that psychopath."

Brooklyn stroked Satin's hair with interest. "I'll bet you guys were scarred for life." The others nodded. "Where did your parents take you?"

"Oh. We moved to a small town called, Matchett. It's in Utah. Ever, heard of it?"

They all shook their heads.

"I went from being totally cool, to being a geek. And it all happened within a few months. One day it was… 'F' you! Then the next day I was humble as a kitten." Satin moaned, smiled, and shook her head. "Finally, I graduated from Matchett High School. But you know what? After we moved, I really got my act together. I threw away the spiked choker, lost the raw attitude, and started to live. Heck, I needed to hide.

I pulled off the black clothing, and skulls, and burned them in a heap. My chains symbolized my rebellion. They literally broke. I breathed a sigh of relief as the weight of them slipped to my feet. I was going to be fine. I missed you guys, but I buried my head in my books. Then one day, I met Davis." She raised her hand to display her bare finger.

The girls screamed with delight. "You're married."

"Where's the ring?" Olivia asked, searching Satin's hand.

"Guys, I can't wear my rings. Little Davis has swollen my hands and feet!"

There were more squeals as the girls gave their sincere wishes for happiness.

"I smell a baby shower," Lace admitted with a grin.

CHAPTER FIVE

Satisfied, Lace folded her arms and admired each of her friends as they chatted away. Pride swelled inside her. She realized her game room was filled with a colorful array of women. Why had she not noticed before? They were all beautiful in their own unique way.

Brooklyn's shiny black hair and almond shaped eyes were the result of mixed cultures. Her mom was Korean and her father was German. Shelda owed her all-weather tan and reddish brown spirals to her Hispanic heritage. Olivia's African American parents had given her skin a creamy brown color. Yara's large green eyes and reddish-brown hair was the results of Irish decedents. Overtones of Native American Indian gave her a ruddy complexion. Satin was a natural blonde, although her parents claimed Columbian ancestry. And of course, she owed her own temper to her Italian father, and her blonde hair to her Nordic mother.

Why had she not noticed in high school? She wasn't a part of the elite crowd, but she still had fun and was regarded as a member of the *Mutt Pack*. The Mutt Pack—a rainbow of cultures. Strong young women, shunned by the elite—Misfits, least likely to succeed. On the contrary, these women had feelings, desires, and dreams.

Yara looked up at Lace with her large round eyes. "What? I know that look. What are you thinking?"

"To be quite honest, Shortcake, I finally realized why they called us the *Mutt Pack*."

"Why?" She chuckled. "Because they thought we were ugly as mutts."

Lace smiled. "No, because we're made up of several highly visible races and cultures."

"Who's a different culture?" Olivia snapped, frowning.

"Don't get radical. No one is attacking you, silly Black woman. Now, pull in your claws. I finally understand why the guys picked on us."

Lace drew a large breath then called, "Timothy. Would you please bring my camera? I want to take a picture of a rainbow."

Brooklyn reached for her cell phone and bantered, "I thought they picked on us because we were dirt poor and part of the Cougar Dance Line. Our parents were too poor to afford cheerleading camp."

Pushing the excited crew together, Lace took several pictures to capture the moment. "I've got video. The first idiot to plaster these on FB will feel my foot up her rear."

CHAPTER SIX

Later, Lace took note that Brooklyn and Yara were sitting side by side on the floor. By the expression on their faces, they were engulfed in a serious conversation.

Lace stood above them. Stamping her feet and clapping, she destroyed the somber atmosphere of their discussion. "I've warned you guys. There will be no serious dialog in this house. You will have fun, darn it! House rules." She placed her hand on her hip. "What are you two hens cackling about anyway?" Scowling, she shook her finger at them. "No serious talks." Lace pointed to Olivia. "You. Get off that cell phone. We've got to get busy. I mean it you guys. Think float."

Yara nibbled a cracker and stared upwards. "I was just telling Brooklyn that we were not prepared for the world when we left Cougar County."

Brooklyn agreed. "Amen sister. We thought the back door of the world ended in Cougar County."

Yara stopped chewing. "I got baptized by fire my very first year at the university. I was *not* ready for the world. I was naive and too trusting."

Lace sat down on the floor in front of the two. "You thought stealing a pair of jeans from Giles's was a big deal."

"Lace," Yara squealed, "we were like, only kids."

Brooklyn shrugged. "Yeah. Our parents couldn't afford nice jeans. I told my mom that the jeans belonged to Shelda, and Shelda told her mom that the jeans belonged to me."

Lace pointed at the two and scolded, "Never mind that, now. I tried to get you guys out of those training panties and into *big girl panties* before college. But no. You guys wouldn't listen." Her voice mellowed. "You guys were like the little sisters I never wanted."

Yara smiled. "Lace you mean every word. But listen to this. See, I had this boss. His named was Barry Banks. This guy was so cruel. Let me tell you what he did. I was working late one night. Right? Everyone was gone home, except me. He glanced across my desk and addressed me like this." Yara tapped violently on the coffee table with her pen. "Tapping on my desk, he says, Miss Dobson—Miss Dobson. Work is over!"

He snapped his finger and I glanced up.

"Miss Dobson. Are you alright?" I was exhausted. Barry pulled down his glasses. "I believe we need to talk about your overtime."

Reluctantly, I started to back up my files. I knew it was time to leave, but I had to get that crap completed. I looked around, then I got pissed. Everyone had left, and I didn't realize *we* were all alone."

Lace interrupted. "What happened, Shortcake? Did he urinate on your precious lunchbox?"

"Lace." Yara narrowed her eyes. "He might as well have." She closed her laptop and pushed it aside. "Ten minutes later, I found myself in Barry's office, seated before his enormous desk. I was so uneasy. He leered over is glasses, and pulled them off his narrow face. With his lips drawn tight, he made a horrific suggestion." She paused. "Miss Dobson. I do know how to lighten your load. I've noticed you've been working late every evening."

"Yes, sir," I replied.

"You do know there is an easier way, right?"

"Mr. Banks. All I know is that hard works pays off."

He got out of his chair and removed his coat. "I've admired how much time you give to cultivating your young body."

"Should I say thank you?"

"It doesn't matter. I know you've been trying to get my attention. That's why you stay late. You know I'll be here. Let's stop playing games."

"I don't know what you mean. I'm only doing my job."

"Come on, Yara. No one works this hard. I could make your life easier. Brenda could pick up the slack. You'll get a substantial raise, and follow me to conferences all over the states."

"Is that proposal supposed to be appetizing to me?"

"Of course." He walked toward my chair. "You want me. Why else would you plump those yummy breasts? My dear, you're so top heavy I wonder how you keep your balance."

"Are you kidding me? You can't say those things to me. That's sexual harassment."

"I recall the good old days when an employer could say anything he pleased. Now, simply because I'm admiring your nice display, you want to report me. You had them surgically altered especially for me, right?"

"No. I didn't do anything for you. Your money can't buy sex from me."

"I have a proposition for you. You know I can make life difficult for you. The last girl in your position quit. That was hardly necessary. All she had to do was scratch my itch. It would have been a rewarding pastime."

"No. I can't believe you're talking liked this."

"You can keep busting that lovely tush of yours for pennies, or you can just lie down, and make so much more."

"Do you know what you're saying?"

"Yes. In fact, you look quite nimble. Were you a gymnast, perhaps?"

"I didn't give in, and Barry Banks made my life hell. He gave everyone's work to me. All employees got extra days off, but I worked like a slave. After that, things got terrible. Barry continued to harass me—taking advantage of his authority. I became so stressed; I started to lose my hair. My nerves were frazzled, and finally, I lost my concentration.

Eventually, I reported Banks for sexual harassment. He couldn't explain that bite mark on the side of his lip. Oh, I left a nasty bruise. Banks called it a weekend golfing accident. Everyone felt sorry for that piece of crap. Of course, he denied all allegations I made against him. Anyway, I moved from his department, but the toad still works there. Men always stick together, don't they? I think it's hardly fair."

Brooklyn gnashed her teeth and shook her head. "Yara, I hope you branded him good! You were strong enough to stand against that idiot. Wonder how many women didn't have the courage to do what you did?"

Lace crossed her legs and sipped her tea. "I'm proud of you, Shortcake. You've got guts."

From behind the sofa, Olivia erupted, "You put on your *big girl panties* that time." She raised her head from the internet and faced Yara. "I didn't think you had that much piss and vinegar in you. You tore a hole in Banks' scheme. Are you sure you don't have a drop of black blood in you somewhere?"

Yara flushed. "That's called an Irish temper, Olivia. And yes, I have one."

CHAPTER SEVEN

Rising from her chair, Lace clapped her hands and stood. "Guys! It's past time to eat. Food on the patio. Hurry! I hate to eat cold food. I'd better call Timothy."

Olivia frowned. "Lace you treat your dad like crap. You act like he's your butler or something?"

As they walked along Satin said, "It's kind of your dad to help, but couldn't you have hired someone else to help him? This place is huge."

Lace's eyes slanted outward in search of Timothy. "Don't let him hear you. He wants to participate in all my affairs."

"So," Satin added. "He's like a savvy father, who helps like a butler?"

"Ah, yeah!" Lace turned in time to see Timothy bringing a pitcher of raspberry tea from the kitchen to the screened-in patio.

Olivia rushed ahead to open the door for him.

As they walked toward the recreation area, Shelda spoke. "I was checking out the media room. It's filled with old movies, girls. Just take your pick." She turned toward Lace. "I didn't know you liked old movies, Lace."

"Old, m...movies?" Lace stammered. "Oh, you mean the old Mae West stuff." She pushed opened the screened door. "It's a long story, Scraps. Someone, other than *Olivia*, told me I had this Mae West Syndrome. I had never heard of it. So, I got a few movies to check it. I watched a few before you guys arrived."

Shelda shrugged. "It's obvious. You've got it, girl. It means you're an assertive '*B*' with attitude. You know — like Mae West. She was years ahead of her time. Did you know she was the first person to say that a homosexual male was a woman's soul trapped in a man's body? I heard she even made a movie about it called, *The Drag*, or something like that.

They even arrested her because they said her films were too racy." Shelda nodded. "Yep, I'd say according to Mae West's outlook on life, she should have been born today. She would have fit in well with our lifestyles. A lot of people didn't know she was more than just a pretty face."

Olivia was already sitting down on the picnic bench. "What are you guys talking about?"

"We were talking about, The Mae West Attitude," Brooklyn replied. "Someone told Lace she had it."

Olivia put on her courtroom face. "As a keen observer of vicious personalities, I must concur."

Throwing up her hands, Lace objected. "Hey. No fair. Mae West is cute and all, but she's bossy, knows what she wants, and won't stop at anything to get it." Lace tried to convince the girls she was different. "She uses men like matches. Once she burns the head off one, she just lights another."

Comfortably seated at the picnic table, they all pointed to Lace. "Mae West Attitude!" they chanted in unison.

Olivia flipped. "Oh, yeah. You've got it, Girl! There's nothing wrong with being assertive."

"Guys, you would think I was Mae West reincarnated. I wonder if she liked children." Lace placed her fingertip thoughtfully to her temple.

"Doubt it!" Yara blasted.

"Think about it, Lace." Olivia picked up an empty plate. "You've got men hanging off you like needles on a Christmas tree. If you shook them all off, you'd weigh about 30 pounds!"

"I do not. Guys. Unfair. You're hurting my image." Lace giggled, horrified by the thought.

Brooklyn reached for the potato salad. "They are right, Lace. You're the kind of woman who would give your employer three months to prove he was worthy of *your* services!"

Laughter filled the screened area. Timothy had obviously overheard their spiteful comments about Lace, his shoulders lurched in laughter. "They are very perceptive," he admitted, pouring the tea. "I knew there was a name for your condition."

"Okay," Lace quipped. "Off my back. I said I'd tolerate your rotten company, not your juvenile insults!"

CHAPTER EIGHT

The BBQ from Everitt's was just as they all remembered. The potato salad was the best ever, the ribs, tender and succulent. Even Timothy joined in on the fun of the evening.

The mood turned more serious and Olivia spoke. "Girls, I need an opinion. Last month I went to California to visit my sister. We went out to dinner. Chase, my old boyfriend, said women turn men into dogs. Do you agree with that?"

Yara lifted her fork. "No way! They *take* their liberties."

"He said we tolerate too much crap from men, therefore we make them dogs."

Shelda shoveled a spoon full of potato salad into her mouth and chewed. "Tell me you're kidding. What kinda jerk is this?"

Apparently, thinking of Chase, Olivia looked across the pool. "He was a handsome jerk who *had* a great job. When I told him about the double standards for men and women, he called me a 'B' in training. After I finished with him, he had a change of heart."

Lace grimaced. "Why, that asinine slug. He didn't want to admit he was wrong."

Shelda scoffed. "See, that's just like a man."

Yara reached for more salad. "Sounds like you guys had quite a conversation. I have to side with you." She wiped her mouth and placed her napkin aside.

Brooklyn closed her eyes and shook her head. "Olivia, we have to stand up — put these skunks in their places."

Lace's lips curled into a devilish grin. "Isn't Chase the one who got away?"

Olivia's eyes widened and her lips parted. "What da?"

Shelda kicked Lace under the table and she winced. "Lace have you seen Steve lately?" She pulled a long rib bone through her lips. "This is, like, so good," she prattled. "I'm so glad you thought of Everitt's. No one makes BBQ like Everitt's. Do you remember when we'd park in front of his restaurant, sit in back of the pick-up, and talk for hours? Everitt always ran us off. He said we were causing too much noise."

"Oh." Brooklyn chimed in. "I guess forty scantily clad girls, didn't work wonders for his business."

"Sure!" Satin interrupted. "We drew the boys, didn't we?"

Lace sang out, "Who didn't buy anything. It's called, obstruction of parking space." She stood up. "It's getting humid out here. If everyone's finished let's go to the media room."

Yara raised her hand. "Little girl's room for me. I'm full of punch."

Shelda pulled her hand out of the air and gazed into her face. "You still don't drink do you?"

Yara shook her head. "No, and I never will." She pushed her picnic chair aside and headed for the bathroom.

Brooklyn hugged herself, and rubbed her arms briskly. "Lace, that was a wonderful meal. I hate to leave this atmosphere of intense bonding, but I just adore that pool. I'll probably take a dip tonight."

Lace had her arms filled with empty cups. "Help yourself. I might even join you."

Brooklyn reached for the cups. "Let me help you with that."

By the time Lace made it to the media room, the girls were already there. Someone had put on an old DVD of a Friday night dance line performance. They were chatting away about old routines and who missed an eight count.

Olivia watched the large screen then screamed in laughter. She pointed at Shelda and snickered. "Girl. You always threw off the entire routine. Then, you would try to catch up by going faster instead of just starting where we were."

Brooklyn sat on the leather sofa. "Yes you did," she recalled, tucking her leg behind her. "I'd take you aside and work with you until I could drop. It wasn't that hard."

"Leave me alone!" Shelda called. "I would get nervous when we got out there. All I could see was thousands and thousands of people, and they were all watching me."

Olivia stood up and mimicked the strut they used to walk onto the field. They all roared in laughter. "And Lace would always walk like this." Holding her hands behind her back, she stuck out her small chest. "Like she was proud to be a Charm. We all knew she was a cheerleader wanna be!"

Lace objected to the cloud of laughter. "Hey! Take that back! I loved being a Charm. We had a great time!"

"But," Brooklyn commented, "when our routine wasn't as racy as the cheerleader's routine, you would just die in disgust. Mother Cougar had to keep telling you that we were actually field entertainment and not cheerleaders."

With a grimace, Lace passed out three yearbooks from the class of 2002. "You had to admit, some of those routines were lame."

Yara walked into the room rubbing lotion on her hands. "But, I liked most of the routines. They were fun! Come on—admit it. We had a great time."

Shelda turned a page in the yearbook. "Yeah, but Lace you were a cheerleader wanna be. You made us ashamed to be a Charm. You always said, just look at us. Our dance is completely dead." Mother Cougar told you we were field entertainment and not a pep squad. We helped the cheerleaders with our pom routines in the stand."

Brooklyn confessed, "They are right. Mother Cougar tried to instill pride in us and you tried to undermine her authority."

With her hands on her hips, Lace stood with mouth agape.

"Like the time she took all the pelvic thrusts out of the routine. She said grandparents and children would be attending that game. Lace secretly made us practice using the thrusts. When we did them on the field, Mother Cougar got called to the Superintendent's office. We all got wrote up."

Olivia leaned forward. "I remember that." She pointed at Lace and said, "Girl, you got us in a lot of trouble that Friday night."

Lace stood in the middle of the floor and declared her innocence. "Am I under attack here? The routine was dead. I wanted to make it lively." She snapped her fingers and wriggled her hips.

"Not funny," Yara scoffed. "We all got demerits. There went my squeaky clean record."

Shelda spoke up. "Yeah! Then Mother Cougar told you that if you wanted to be a cheerleader, help yourself. That was our junior year. You tried out, right. Honey eight years of ballet didn't help you. You're a dancer. Cheerleading is poppy and frisky."

Lace chided, "I was poppy and frisky. I made the squad."

Brooklyn turned another page in her book. "Yes, you did make the squad. Why didn't you stay?"

Lace blushed. "Hey! I missed you knuckleheads! I guess I was just born to be a Mutt."

Shelda reared up. "That's not what I heard. I heard you faked an injury."

Lace shook her head. "One plus one is not three. I faked an injury so I could get back with you guys. The cheerleaders didn't like me that much. Not that I gave a sh—" Lace looked at Yara. "Yara, save me please. These Cougars are tearing me apart."

They shook their fingers at Lace. "Shame on you!"

Shelda yelled, "Yeah, you sell out!"

"Girls. You are my guests. Now, shut up and get over it."

Olivia nodded. "She's right." She got up and gave Lace a big hug. "I love you, girl. And I'm glad you invited us here for a Special Cougar Charm Reunion."

Brooklyn pondered. "You know, I kinda miss Kayleigh. She would really enjoy this event. I hope she's okay."

Lace twirled her wrist. "She was invited, you know. It was her choice not to come."

Olivia playfully smacked Lace on the head. "Don't be so hard on her. She had to work. Some of us have to work for a living, you know."

CHAPTER NINE

As the evening waned, the girls laughed over yearbook pictures and DVDs made of their routines. They teased anyone who was off count. Lace called for Timothy. "Timothy would you bring us something to drink? I'm dying for a smoke." She stood in front of the large flat screen, blocking their view. "I'm going to the sun porch for a smoke. Anyone want to join me?"

Satin gazed around the room. "Why don't you try an electronic cigarette? No one smokes anymore, Lace."

Yara stood up. "I'll join you."

Lace seemed surprised. "Why, Miss Polly Purebred—are you smoking now?"

"No, but I work around people who do smoke. I don't mind."

* * * * *

They walked onto the porch, and Lace lit up. She took a deep pull from her cigarette and said, "I've been waiting for this all evening. With the aroma of BBQ in the air, Lace sat down on her favorite patio chase. "Do you want Timothy to bring you something? Oh, that's right. You're a non-drinker. You do that alcohol and drug counseling thing, right."

"Yep. I'm still at it." Yara sat down on the opposite chase.

As Lace spoke, white clouds of smoke rushed from her lips. "What started you on that path? I thought you wanted to become a chef."

"Well, let's just say the stars had other plans for me."

Lace tucked her feet beneath her as she sat upright on the chase. She thumped her ashes into a clean ashtray. "What happened? It had something to do with your sister, right?"

"Yeah. She died from a drug overdose."

"I heard about that. That really sucks."

Gazing absently across the yard, Yara seemed to reminisce. "Right then, I changed my mind about my profession and decided to become an alcohol and drug counselor. My sister died in my arms that night. She needed counseling and medication." Yara lowered her voice. "I still blame myself for her death.

She can't fight, but I'll fight for her cause. Hopefully, I can save someone from this horrible fate. I can't help it. My heart goes out to addicts. Especially addicts who want so desperately to recover, but can't get their heads above the water. A part of me died with Jen that day."

After Yara finished her statement, she wrung her hands. Lace felt her grief. Although she had a tough exterior, she wiped back a tear. "How can you talk about it? It's kinda like when I lost my parents, only worse. I walked out of the wreckage that day, but they didn't. My life changed forever. If it wasn't for Timothy, I guess I would have blown my brains out by now." She nodded. "He keeps me together."

Yara nodded and acknowledged, "So, Timothy is actually your guardian?"

Avoiding the question, Lace noticed that she had smoked three cigarettes. "Oh crap! I'm trying to cut back. See what you did. Now, I can't have another smoke until…" She looked at her watch. "Ten o'clock tomorrow. Darn!"

"I thought you were wearing a patch. I'm sorry." Yara smiled.

"Don't be sorry, kid. I really do need to quit. Hardly anyone with any sense smokes anymore anyway." She stood up and brushed ashes from her skirt. "Let's go back inside, huh? They've probably called in male strippers by now."

CHAPTER TEN

Once inside, Lace and Yara discovered that the conversation had also taken on a different tone. The DVDs were over, and the girls sat in a huddle, chatting away.

Lace called out. "What's going on here? We're supposed to be making plans for our float. This sound like a serious conversation and serious conversations are forbidden this weekend."

"Guilty," Shelda yelled, holding her hand in the air. "Now that I've eaten everything in sight, the only other thing I can do with my mouth is talk." She chuckled, holding her fat tummy. Shelda placed her tea on the floor. "Since Lace and Yara interrupted me, I'm going to start over so they can catch up. Long story short. When I first met that idiot…"

Yara's eyes grew large. "Just get to the juicy part," she encouraged.

Shelda ignored her. "I've got to tell you the first part, so you'll understand what happened." She looked over Yara's head and drew her lips tightly. "I didn't interrupt you when you were talking about that Barry Banks jerk."

Lace sat down beside Shelda. "Never mind that bull crap. Shut up and just tell us. The suspense is killing me."

Shelda cut her eyes at Yara, but calmed down. "Well, we had hardly dated three months when this piece of man beef came unglued at the seams. He was so pretty. Perfect brows. A mouth that makes goose bumps rise on your back—a voice like that suave British guy on television. I knew there was something wrong, but if you saw him—O.M.G. Olivia pulled him up on the internet. The man was actually a model. ...made really good money. I had no idea what he was doing in *my* small town. We met at the men's clothing store. After dating for a while, I discovered it was all a front. A front, I tell you! This guy, Storm, was gay. How could he have tricked me?

Then I realized the signs were always there. He was neat as a pin. Kept his apartment clean, and wore the most impeccable clothes I'd ever seen. Girls. I swore men were flirting with him, but he said it was all in my head.

Beth Wedding

When I caught him in his apartment with his real lover, I wanted to gag. Storm had put my life in danger. Unprotected sex.

"Shelda," he pleaded, "I'm trying to change my life. Please forgive me."

"I want to believe you, Storm. What kind of joke is this? You could have been honest from the start."

When he approached me with those blue eyes, I almost melted. They were the most sensual eyes I'd ever seen. He grabbed me by my shoulders, and shook me. "I want you Shelda. I want a wife. I want kids."

"I can't do this, Storm." I pushed him away. "I can't be your savior. Who knows when you'd decide I wasn't man enough for you."

"Please. Shelda. I promise; I can change. I want to change—I need to change."

With tears in my eyes, I looked at Storm. Still, his perfect face intrigued me. "I can't help you, Storm. I love you too much. It would never work."

Partially dressed, he had fallen to his knees. Holding his head in shame, he groaned, engaged my eyes, then whispered, "I'm sorry. I'm so sorry."

Dirty Lace

Humiliated, Storm sat on the side of the bed and held his beautiful head in his hands. Then, with a knot in my gut, I walked away from the prettiest man I'd ever known. Guys. He was simply stunning.

The next time I got serious about a guy, I made sure he was a manly man. Believe me, I was finished with the pretty boys. Give me a big gut man, who drinks beer, scratches his furry butt, farts, and burps."

Olivia scoffed. "Perhaps you should have given him a chance. He sounded so sincere."

"Olivia. He was having sex. With a man. Hello!"

Alarmed, Lace got up from the floor. "Eeew! See, that's why I keep things loose when it comes to men. They're all the same — gay or straight. I prefer having someone I can use when necessary, then toss away, like used toilet paper."

Brooklyn spoke up. "She's referring to Scott, you guys. Have you seen him? I'll bet he's fine as frog's hair."

Yara laughed. "Now, that's pretty fine. When do we meet him?"

Lace shuddered. "If I keep listening to such explicit experiences, I might check his bottom to make sure he's a boy. He'll be here shortly. But, not to meet you guys." She smiled deceitfully.

Olivia pouted. "I feel cheated. Shelda never did get to the good part about meeting her new husband, and that whole scenario."

Shelda placed her fingers to her lips. "I'll save that for later. I promise."

Olivia scooted toward her. "You guys try to stay married. People don't even try to stay together anymore. Our parents fought to stay a family. It's just too easy to give up. "

Shelda winced. "Honey. You have no idea how hard I've fought."

CHAPTER ELEVEN

Lace slapped her forehead. "Guys! How could I have forgotten? Wedding Bells! Brooklyn is getting married soon!"

Brooklyn blushed. "Lace introduced us, guys."

Yara spoke up, "She never introduced me to any of her male friends."

Shelda grew excited. "Oh-my- gosh, Brooklyn, it's about time you got out."

Satin stood up and waddled toward the restroom. "Give us all the details, but don't start until I get back, okay." Satin held her back as if it ached. Waddling, she struggled toward a nearby restroom.

Yara called after Satin. "Do you need any help, Scraps?"

"Well, I didn't need any help making him." She patted her round tummy. "So, I guess I don't need any help now."

"Satin, get real," Lace quipped. "You're having a rug-rat. Let someone help you." She turned toward the girls. "… still stubborn, I see."

Brooklyn stroked her throat. "Lace, could we have more of that raspberry tea. I'm so parched, I could absolutely blow away."

Shelda leaned toward Brooklyn. "Don't leave out a thing."

Brooklyn started to speak. "Guys — you guys. It's really no big deal. I don't want to talk right now."

Olivia threatened, "It's your turn, Brooklyn and you'd better start talking. Otherwise, we'll start cutting out little tissue flowers for a darn float!"

"We can cut and talk, too." Lace gathered art supplies she'd placed in a plastic crate. "After all, that's why we're here." Lace gave Yara and Olivia each a pair of scissors, and construction paper with large flowers printed on them.

"What's this crap," Olivia asked, turning the orange paper over in her hand.

Lace shook her hips as if they were driven by music. "Didn't I tell you guys the theme for the parade is the 70's?"

"No," they replied in unison. "You neglected to tell us that part."

"This could take forever," Yara whined, looking over the mountain of work.

"Yeah," Shelda huffed, folding her arms. "I did want to have a little fun this weekend."

"Look at all these flowers!" Olivia pointed to the flowers scattered all over the floor. "We'll never get finished."

Satin finally returned and eased herself down in a chair. "What'd I miss?"

Brooklyn ran her fingers through her hair. "Nothing, sweetie. I waited for you, as requested. Unlike some people I know, who's names- I will not mention."

Timothy brought Brooklyn a special glass of raspberry tea with crushed ice and a slice of orange. "Thanks, Timothy. This should hit the spot." She started to sip, but almost finished the entire glass. "Now, that was fantastic!"

She blotted her thin lips, then chose a pink flower to cut. "Let's get busy. If we all pitch in, we'll be finished within the hour."

"So," Satin insisted, "are you going to tell us about Winston?" Brooklyn stared at Satin, then Lace. "Lace, why don't you tell them about Scott, first."

"Scott." They looked at each other. "Who is this mystery man?"

"Woah." Lace shot back. She pointed her shears at each of them. "Brooklyn, that's my own personal business. How dare you. You hens volunteered to share your misery. I'm not talking."

Olivia picked up another flower and started to trim. "We've been sharing stories. So, why can't you?"

"Step off, Olivia!" She opened her scissors and closed them with a violent snap. "You guys haven't been talking about anything. Now, you want to talk about sex. A lady never tells." The doorbell rang and Lace sprang to her feet. "Besides! Let's put this mess down for a while and take a dip in the pool. We can finish after that." Lace disappeared behind the sofa as she picked up cut flowers.

"I could use a dip." Yara stretched her arms.

Olivia spoke up, "Girl, me too." She placed her scissors on the floor. "Let's get naked. That is, if you guys aren't afraid I'll turn the water into chocolate with my sweet brown skin."

"Chocolate," Brooklyn mused, leaning against the sofa. "Olivia you are so weird." She placed her materials on the floor. "I'm in!" She shook her finger at Olivia. "Although, not naked! I'm not into that kinky stuff." Olivia stroked Brooklyn's back. "I was only kidding."

Shortly afterward, Lace stood up holding several terribly trimmed flowers. "You guys are awful. Just look at this mess. How are we going to turn this into something beautiful?"

Timothy came to the game room. He was followed by an older male whose face brightened when he saw the room filled with beautiful women.

Lace placed the flowers aside and dusted her hands. "Guys! This is Madison. My Accountant."

Madison walked over to introduce himself to the girls. One by one, they gave their name and nodded. "It is a pleasure to meet you, ladies. I only need a moment of your good friend's time. Then, I'll be on my way."

"Why don't you join us?" Lace pointed to the other women. "We were about to launch a nasty attack on the pool."

"Oh, I couldn't." Madison blushed. "You guys go ahead and have fun."

Stroking Madison's arm Lace informed, "Madison is an old friend of the family. He's been around since—I mean, since I was born."

"Well, I have a keen interest in Lace's

welfare."

Olivia shook her hand as if she had touched something hot. She whispered to Satin. "Looks like Mr. Accountant has more on his mind than her welfare."

Satin elevated her gaze. "I do agree, girlfriend. I do agree."

Hearing their whispers, Lace blasted, "See, that's why I don't like a bunch of females around. I never felt guilty before." Then she kidded, "Darn, now I've got to get a man for each of you." She busted into laughter, then slapped Madison on the rear. "Get dressed. I want you outside on a beach chair, right now!"

Madison, obviously embarrassed by her affectionate display, shrugged. "Okay. If you insist, Lace."

Madison was a die-hard bachelor. He was over sixty years old. Apparently, he loved the way Lace teased him. As he scaled the stairs, Lace called, "Get those white buns upstairs and into a bathing suit. You need some sun, man!"

Yara shivered as she watched the unusual production. "Why do you play with him like that? Show him some respect."

"Kiss my butt, Yara. Madison isn't as innocent as he looks."

Dirty Lace

Brooklyn was the first to the pool area. She lazed in a lounger and basked in the sun. "Mmmm. This is so nice."

Shelda sauntered out to the pool. "You guys, I swear. This house is enormous. How many bedrooms does it have?"

Lace, who rubbed sunscreen on her legs, answered absently, "Oh, about sixteen."

Olivia pulled her sheer robe together and sat down on the chair near Brooklyn. "And, why do we need this much room. You might as well have rented an entire hotel."

A devilish smile curled Lace's lips. "Oh. I needed this much room to accommodate bitc — " Timothy passed out towels. He grunted, breaking her next word in half.

"I hear you, Timothy." She frowned. "I was trying to say witches, but it just wasn't coming out right."

"Oh, that's real funny, Lace," Olivia sassed. "When are we going to meet that little cookie you call, Scott?"

Brooklyn pulled down her sunglasses, peering at Lace. "What did I miss? Did someone say we have cookies?"

Shelda grinned. "One of us has a cookie,"

she said, biting her strawberry in a seductive manor.

Lace crunched a piece of ice from her drink. "Is it a crime to get satisfied every now and then?"

Timothy cleared his throat.

"Okay." Lace admitted, "Four or five times a week, but no more."

"Oool," the girls crowed.

"I didn't get that much attention when I was trying to get pregnant with Melissa." Brooklyn pushed her shades back upon her nose.

Lace poured another glass of tea. "Speaking of which. Did you call your little munchkins? Cell phones are not prohibited."

Brooklyn smiled. "They're fine. Nana has them. They dearly love their Nana."

Olivia reached for a yogurt and spoon. "Someone is trying to change the subject." She walked up to Lace, licking her spoon. "I said, when do we meet this guy?"

Madison approached the pool. He tossed a large towel across his shoulders and said, "Looks like she has your foot to the fire, Ms. Garnett."

"Oh, shut up, you." Lace scoffed. "You're

just angry because I didn't let you into my world." She stroked her curvaceous body.

Yara was kicking her feet in the water, but she winced. "Lace!"

Madison sighed wishfully. "Ms. Garnett. I don't deny that you are very seductive. After all, I am a man. I take pleasure in the female anatomy. For instance, all of these beautiful ladies bouncing around me are very much to my liking."

Satin caught Madison by the arm, then rubbed her tummy with the other hand. "Thank you Madison." She gawked at the others, sticking out her tongue. "See, I'm still sexy, large belly and all."

"Well, show it to Davis. We don't want to see it." Olivia teased. "Lace. How did you meet this Scott?"

Lace put down her glass and picked up her cigarette case. "I think I need a smoke."

"No way." Shelda retort. "No smoking. It's your turn. We've been sharing our dirt."

Lace receded. "Okay. Actually, it was Madison who was responsible for Scott."

They turned and looked at Madison. He shrugged. "What?"

She shook her finger at Madison. "Don't

give me that, *what* bull, Madison." She opened a bottle of water and began to pour. "If you must know, Madison had a crush on me at one time."

"Is that true Madison?" they asked.

Madison nodded. "Yes. I admitted to that earlier. Ms. Garnett is a very sensual woman. I would do anything to be near her. A man would have to be dead not to desire her."

"Thank you Madison." She blew him a kiss. "And, I didn't pay him to say that."

Yara looked at Shelda, Shelda looked at Olivia, Olivia looked at Brooklyn. They all looked at Lace. In unison they said, "Mae West Attitude!"

Brooklyn was sitting with eyes closed. "Don't give us that mush, Lacy. How did you meet Scott?" As she soaked up the sun, she slid her arm down by her side. "Don't take any short cuts. I want the scenic route."

Lace sat back down and lit a cigarette. "You guys make my butt hurt. Well, if you must know, I was on vacation. Our vacations always included Madison. If I didn't find a date, I had dinner with Timothy or Madison. Well, this time, Madison and I were sitting by the pool and out of the blue Madison propositioned me.

"When are you going to stop sharing your

nectar from man to man and marry me, Lace Garnett? After all, haven't you noticed my temples are getting whiter. And you, although quite a sensual young woman, can't bargain with time forever."

I lifted my eyes from beneath the brim of my large straw hat and pulled down my dark shades. I gazed into Madison's gentle eyes. With a sweep of my lashes, I smiled as if thinking about his question. Teasing him, I placed my middle finger around the rim of my glass, then licked my fingers. "Madison," I said. "I adore you, and I appreciate your candor. But, in all honesty I feel you should be aware of one fact. I am as old as I want to be." I drew closer to Madison and in a whisper mouthed, "and as young as I dare to be." With that said, I blew a kiss in his direction on the tropical breeze."

Brooklyn butted in. "Lace is such a drama queen. She has to tell everything in such a theatrical way."

Yara came to her defense. "I like the way she tells things. She wouldn't be Lace if she did it any other way."

"Thank you. I've never been typical about anything." She turned to address Timothy. "Timothy wasn't there. Anyway, a distressing yowl from a child in the hotel's pool caught our attention. A young mother slipped into the pool to retrieve her youngster's floating toy."

Madison turned his attention back to me, his eyes sweeping over the sun-siphoned moistness forming in the center of my breast. His eyes drifted downward to my colorful sarong and my bronzed legs crossed femininely at the knee. The shimmer of a gold bracelet lying against my ankle added to my mystic."

"Lace," he sighed. "We've been playing this game for five years. You use me like an expensive toy, My Dear."

My stomach quickened. "Madison," I whined. "How could you say such a thing?" I turned my face from his in playful disagreement. "Is it wrong to enjoy your familiar company? I always love my vacations with you, Madison. I'm pretty sure I knew your intentions."

"That's nonsense, Lace. I did not intend to fall in love with you. Why, you were just a child in my eyes."

"Well, I'm not a child anymore, Madison. There is nothing to stop you. Your dedication went far beyond accounting. You can stop looking after me, now."

"I can't. Don't you see, Lace. After all

these years you've become a part of me. I can't lie and say, quite frankly that you don't appeal to me in the worst way."

"Oh, Madison." Reaching out, I stroked the gray tufts of hair on his bare chest with my fingers. "I love life. I love people. I don't want to get deeply involved with anyone." I placed my hand across his, and searched his dim eyes for signs of acknowledgment. "You understand, don't you, Madison?"

"I'll try. But, I can't help myself. I loved your mother from afar, and you're the very image of her. If your father had only known he would have..."

"...never trusted you as his accountant?"

"Precisely!"

"Why didn't you date and marry mother first? After all, you did introduce them?"

"Oh, Lace. By the time I knew I loved your mother your father was escorting her down the aisle."

He pounded the metal patio table. "They looked so happy. I grew more distant by the day."

About this time, a tanned, muscular male, clad in a leopard thong walked past us as we talked. I shifted my head ever so slightly. My attentive eyes followed his firm rear down the paved walkway and toward the lobby. Madison strained his eyes to see what was so interesting. "So, that's all you want in a man…a leopard loincloth? Indeed, Lace."

He frowned to show his distaste for the stingy fabric, then shrugged his shoulders as if a cold shiver overtook him.

"Yes, Madison," I quipped playfully. "…a leopard loincloth, a pleasing rear, a sincere heart, and a decent paying job."

Madison lowered his eyes in disappointment. "I knew I could never…"

"Don't try to compete with other men, it isn't necessary. You'll always have a special place in my heart. I keep my feelings for you in a place no man could possibly earn."

"I know you're trying to make me feel better, and I appreciate your kindness."

I slipped my feet back into my wedge sandals. "I'm going up to my room now. Shall I meet you for dinner?"

"Anytime, Lace. Even if I'd eaten an entire banquet, I'd still have room for you."

I smiled affectionately, attempting to replace my sunglasses. I squinted in the mid-day sun as I stood—my sarong blowing about my body. I kissed Madison on the cheek. "Thank you Madison, lunch was marvelous."

Madison interrupted Lace's conversation. "I watched Lace as she slowly walked away—confident shoulders erect, the naughty rhythm of her curvaceous hips harassing me. As she walked along the pool's side, she held the brim of her straw hat pinched between her fingers. Unexpectedly, she removed it. Her silken blonde hair took flight on the mellow breeze."

Satin moaned aloud. "O. M. G. Madison. Sounds like you're in love."

Madison spoke without hesitation. "I don't deny that."

Lace grew peeved. "Guys, let me finish. We've got things to do today."

"We're sorry," Brooklyn apologized.

Yara massaged her shoulders and moaned. "Go ahead. This sounds so luscious!"

Annoyed, Lace pulled down her glasses. Her piercing green eyes singled out each female. "Do you want me to talk or not? No more interruptions, okay."

Lace pushed her glasses back upon her nose. "Where was I? Oh, yeah. At seven o'clock, I stood at the hotel's dining room door. Dressed in a short, backless sundress, I had not anticipated such a crowd. Locating Madison was going to be difficult. I hailed a waiter and immediately a young man greeted me with a cheery hello.

"Well, hi, yourself. I'm looking for a gentleman who would be sitting alone, perhaps in a dark suit."

The waiter's eyes brighten. "Yes. He's seated in the rear, Ms. Garnett. Please, follow me."

When I reached the rear, Madison was nowhere to be found. However, the waiter did escort me to the table where *the loincloth* was seated. He was alone and wearing a dark suit. There, I stood — my curiosity piqued with the trauma of seeing the loincloth fully clothed. He was more handsome than before, if that were logically possible. I smiled. Then, shaking my head with confusion, I turned toward the waiter. "I'm sorry, but this isn't the gentleman I was referring to."

The waiter was a little surprised that he could have been mistaken. He addressed the seated man. "Sir. Is this not the young lady you are waiting for?"

The man seated at the table flashed a

broad smile. "Yes. She's the one. Thank you." He gazed upward into my blushing face.

"Please Lace, have a seat."

I was puzzled. Raising both brows, I inquired, "And you are—

Ignoring my question the man arched a debonair brow in response to my prodding. "Madison will be along shortly."

"Pardon me. What did you say?" At the mention of Madison's name, I sat down, though, a little suspicious. "Wait just a minute. What's going on here?" I took in his bright sincere eyes against his sun-kissed skin.

"It's no joke, Lace." He paused. His baritone voice reverberated in my well-trained ear. "Why don't we order coffee and I'll tell you all about it."

"Yes, this should be interesting." After removing my cell, I laid my clutch aside. There was no message. I crossed my arms and tilted my head. "Let's say you share the goods, huh stud?"

He grinned and raised two fingers in the air. Immediately, the server reached for the coffee pot and two elegant cups. As the man grew silent, his manliness grew more pronounced in my presence. "Madison is an old family friend," he finally admitted.

I drummed my fingers. "Really?" With palms under my chin, I leaned forward and whispered, "Besides being incredibly sexy- and strikingly handsome you are…"

"Oh, I'm sorry." Seeming humiliated, he chuckled. "How rude of me. My name is Scott. Scott Sutton."

"Scott, huh?" My brow twitched at the sonorous tone of it. "Quite a common name."

"I've heard all the jokes. Unless you have some new ones to add to my collection, we can retire that subject."

"Sure." I sighed, fidgeted with the snap on my clutch, then I looked toward the doorway. "You did say Madison would be along shortly?"

"Please, relax." His pleasantly puzzling eyes drew a frown. "Now, you're making me uncomfortable. I've never practiced being a male in waiting. I've got to admit; when Madison asked me to wait for you, I was a bit apprehensive about this entire ordeal. However, I feel it will be safe for us to place an order now."

Again, I looked toward the doorway. "I think I should call up to Madison's room. It's so unlike him to be late for anything." I sipped at the sweet, scented coffee the server slipped between us during our light conversation.

"Perhaps he's…" he cleared his throat, "busy."

I was growing antsy but managed a mistrustful calm. "How could he possibly be busy?"

Scott placed his cup on the table and stated, "He's with my Mom."

"Your—"

"Mom."

"Why that rascal." Boy was I surprised.

"Now, will you relax? He only wanted me to keep you company until they arrived."

I relaxed. "Okay. Now, show me that sexy smile again. I want to record it for future reference."

He blushed and displayed deep masculine dimples. "Madison said you were a valorous woman of few words."

I looked him over once again. His charming personality grew on me with each vanishing minute. Holding my cup with both hands, I inquired in my unique way. "Your shoulders are enormous. Do you have your suits specially tailored?"

Tugging at his lapels, he admitted shamefully, "I don't, but I should." Scott started to confess. "Lace, if I tell you that I've always wanted to meet you—you wouldn't take it as a come-on, would you?"

"Of course not. You just have exceptional taste in females. You know, there is something familiar about you." I laid my finger aside my chin and pondered.

"Actually I grew up down the street from you. I'm Little Scott."

"Get out, Little Scott. Excuse me, but you aren't little any more. You've got to be, what—twenty-seven, twenty-eight?"

"And you're twenty-nine." The intelligence in his eyes intensified over the fragrant light of the flickering candle. "You live at 202 Garnett Lane. Your favorite color is old money. You love Antique cars, with an extraordinary passion for old Thunderbirds."

"Excuse me. What did you say?" I raised a suspicious brow. "Who gave you that information, precious? I don't advertise on the internet."

Scott drew in his breath and took a sip of his coffee. "Okay, time to get truthful." He gazed about the room as if expecting someone besides Madison. "Please don't get angry with me. It took me a long time to get to this point, so promise me that you won't be judgmental. Promise?"

"Of course I won't judge you — you silky devil."

"Trust me; I'm no fruitcake, okay. But, is it wrong to worship a female. You've got this unbelievable, modern-day Mae West thing going, and it drives me wild. Like many other men, I've been a devoted clown for you since we moved to Cougar County."

I couldn't believe it. My eyes narrowed in disbelief. Sincerity glazed his voice. Hearing the combination of voice quality and raw sexuality, I recoiled.

"I tried every way possible to meet you, but I just didn't feel comfortable in your circle of friends. Every chance I got, I read everything I could about you. I even purchased your high school year book so I could be a silent part of your life."

"Mae West, huh? Well, that's more than incredible, Scott. Why didn't you just come right out with it?" I demanded. "Am I contaminated or something?"

"I guess you could say I didn't want to seem like some sort of weirdo. I hoped destiny would make our paths cross. I hate to admit this, but I'm a bit awkward in situations like this. I just didn't want to come off sounding like a crackpot. And, being reserved, I didn't get out much until after my divorce.

"It's not what you're thinking, Lace. I married a woman who—well, was pleasing, and quite likable. However, I was never quite contented with her. We were more like friends than lovers. Just good friends. If I saw her with another man, it wouldn't faze me at all. I knew that I didn't feel as I should for her. So, I set her free." He leaned back in his chair. His enormous shoulders slumped as his voice softened. "And, I never forgot you, Lace. You were my distant love, my fantasy, and dream lover. You were the deception I lived for."

With mouth agape, I sat glowing in the shower of his unreserved splendor. "I—I don't know what to say, Scott. I guess there are no words to describe this extraordinary revelation."

Scott's voice brightened. "Once you had a birthday party. Your twentieth." He lowered his eyes and admitted, "I crashed your party. I just wanted to be in your presence. There were so many people there—I didn't feel comfortable. But, I did ask you to dance with me."

Lace strained to remember the incident. "I

just don't recall."

"I remember. You said, I'm sorry little boy, not right now. But, when you grow up, come up, and see me sometime."

"I couldn't believe I had repeated that ancient Mae West line."

The girls stopped the conversation and slapped palms together. "See, we told you!"

"That's why I don't like a bunch of females around. They are such clucks." She busted into laughter. "Back to my story.

Scott' attention was drawn near the doorway. "Look." He nodded. "There's Madison and my Mom."

Lace turned toward the doorway. Madison was arm in arm with a lovely woman who looked to be about fifty-five. Proudly, Madison strutted toward the table, periodically taking in the beautiful specimen on his arm. When he reached the table, he stopped. "Lace, I would like for you to meet Ann." He gazed into Ann's eyes. "We're old friends."

I was puzzled, but elated. "Why you rascal. Are you having a good time?"

Madison chuckled, a devilish twitter echoed deep in his throat. "Are you having a good time, My Dear? I see that you've finally captured the leopard-skinned trophy. However, this one is not riddled with bullet holes. I'll bet he took you on a merry chase."

I was a bit embarrassed, but I pulled out the chair next to her. "Ann, please sit down." I offered Ann my hand. "May I say, it's certainly a pleasure to meet you."

Ann sat down, her dress shimmering against the flickering candle. "And I see you've met my son, Scott."

I knew my eyes were sparkling. "Yes I have, and he's quite a guy. ...sensitive, kind, thoughtful..."

"and rich." Ann beamed.

"Mother, please," Scott begged, seemingly exasperated.

"Well it's true, son." She grasped his hand and gave it an affectionate squeeze. "We're among friends. I can toot my own horn. Can you believe it? The first thing he wanted to do was take me on vacation. This island is lovely. Don't you agree, Madison?"

"Why yes, Dear, and it's getting better every hour."

"Oh you." She giggled like a teenager then snuggled her nose against his. "Madison and I are going dancing for a while." They both prepared to leave. "Don't wait up, Scott."

After I watched them disappear into the crowd, I turned my attention back to Scott. "They look like quite a pair."

Scott gazed down at his empty cup and whispered. "I would like to become a pair, Lace. That is—" he gazed deep into my eyes, "if you would allow yourself the agony of getting to know me."

"After all you've told me, I would be less than a lady if I didn't at least call you, or spend a little more time getting to know the real you."

"Even if I have one more confession?" A hopeful expression quieted his smile.

I sipped my tepid coffee and almost strangled on his sentence. "There is no way there could be more to this. But, I'd love to hear it," I conceded, clearing my throat.

Scott hailed a waiter. "Well, off comes the clothing, and out with the truth. This trip was no accident. I've known Madison for years. I knew you came here regularly. You've done so for many years. After my dad died, I thought it would be good to bring mother here for a vacation.

"And you arranged to get Madison and Ann together? What a brilliant plan."

"I hoped it would be a packaged deal. Hopefully, Madison is pleased with Mom, and hopefully you'll give me a few moments of your time."

I shook my head. "Scott, I'm slightly older than you. Yet, I find you strangely appealing. You're like a crazed fan I don't deserve. How could I deny you equal time? I'm simply flattered. It's been years since anyone truly found me appealing." I reached out and grasped Scott's hand, giving it a gentle squeeze. "That is to say — your sincerity is confusing. I know you're not a nut, but I do feel a bit anxious." Our eyes met in agreement.

"I understand, Lace. Take your time, I've waited this long. A few more months won't kill me. The main thing is; I finally made a step toward getting to know you, whether you shun me or not. Thanks for the opportunity."

I sighed. "You're a sweetheart for being understanding. I really do appreciate all the trouble you've gone through to make this happen. You're incredibility sensitive," I crooned. "Your heart is good, you're handsome. You're all I could ever want in a man."

Then jokingly, I sputtered, "Next time you have the urge to crash another party, use a bull-dozer. I'll bet that'll get my attention."

Madison stood up and took a bow. "And the rest is history."

The girls sat with mouths agape. Shelda's brows went up. "He was sort of a stalker, right?"

Olivia tapped her on the shoulder. "No, Sweetie. He wasn't a stalker. That is called L O V E."

Brooklyn swatted an insect. "See, I told you, Lace. Even in high school, you had this-sexually aggressive attitude. Scott confirmed that theory."

"Step off! I told you hens what you wanted to know." Lace took a long swallow of her drink.

"But there was no sex." Satin reminded them.

Yara stroked the patio table. "You don't always need to have sex when true love is involved." Looking into Satin's eyes, she added. "You can be in love with a person and never have sexual relationships."

"So, do we get to meet him tonight?" Olivia asked.

Lace looked at Madison. "You can't. He's out of town."

Brooklyn stroked her insect bite. "Is that

true, Madison?"

Lace recoiled, "Stop! We need to think about the task before us."

"Sure!" Olivia stormed. "We'll think about the task and you'll be thinking about Scott."

Lace snapped her fingers. "One hour guys. I say you hens should shower, get dressed, and meet in the game room.

Satin yawned. "I can't keep my eyes open."

"You're excused to take a nap, Satin. But, the rest of these witches must work for their supper. Timothy and Madison learned to use scissors in kindergarten, so they're included, too."

Madison frowned. "You're a hard woman, my dear, but, I've a five o'clock appointment. It's getting late."

"Then, you're excused, too." Lace drove the pack of tired women. "Up, you lazy girls."

Shelda rebelled, speaking to Olivia. "Sounds just like our old dance line days, huh?"

Olivia agreed. "Once a captain, always a captain."

* * * * *

Two hours later, the girls finally met in

the media room. Lace's home theater was awesome. One entire wall housed a movie screen to make the most of viewing pleasure. The girl's reactions revealed their liking. Satin had kicked back and was enjoying a carefully selected movie. "Now, this is the life."

Lace stood in the doorway. Her hands were perched firmly on her hips. "I didn't fly your enormous butts all the way out here to watch movies. Let's get busy."

"But, we are busy," Yara confessed. "I've cut out this many." She held up a tall stack of flowers.

Olivia raised her stack. "Here's mine."

Brooklyn simply raised her large stack.

"Oh." Lace stammered. "I guess I'm the only one who hasn't cut her share."

They gazed at each other in amazement. "Nah—ya think?" Shelda acknowledged, turning back to her task. When the patterns were finished, Lace showed them how to make the large colorful flower. As they finished, they tossed them into large boxes. "Tomorrow," Lace said. "We'll go out and purchase our 70's outfits."

Yara glowered. "Didn't you bring anything with you?"

Shrugging, Lace admitted, "I could have, but it'll be more fun to go shopping."

Brooklyn clapped her hands. "I say we shop."

"Fine with me," they all agreed.

As the night wore on, everyone relaxed. Fatigue became a grave issue. The giant clock over the mantle swore it was 9:30, however, Lace's body felt more like two in the morning.

"Guys," Olivia confessed. "I can hardly keep my eyes open. I've got to move around."

"Me, too." Yara got up from the sofa and stretched.

Lace urged, "Let's walk outside for a minute. The yard is gated, you know."

"Yes, Ms. West. We hear and we obey," Olivia recited.

Lace took them through the garden. They loved the colorful array of flowers in the moonlight. After sitting on the swing for a while, they finally emerged half-eaten by mosquitoes. Each woman was scratching and terribly unhappy.

"You wimps!" Lace decreed. "I'll get some ointment. Just sit down in the game room. It's a good thing Scraps is already asleep."

As Lace ascended the stairs, she heard

Brooklyn's voice. "You guys know how persuasive Lace can be. It was about two years after Carter's death. It didn't matter that I was in mourning, Lace felt like it was time for me to start dating."

Lace threw up her hands. From the stairs she yelled, "Stop talking. I'm not there to defend myself."

When Lace returned, it was obvious the conversation was still going. She shook the first aid cream at Brooklyn. "I told you bats to stop talking, didn't I?" She smacked Brooklyn on the shoulder. "I asked Brook how she could just give up after a few dates didn't go well."

Brooklyn squirted some cream onto her fingertip, displaying her large diamond ring. "I can remember it like it was yesterday. I wouldn't listen to anything Lace had to say. We were shopping that day."

"Yeah," Lace said, irritated. "I was trying to tell her about Winston, and she told me I sucked at picking mates."

Brooklyn rubbed the ointment on her arm. "Yeah. I did give her a hard time. I'm sorry. I just wasn't ready. This is what really happened. We had just finished the mall. It was hot that day and Lace was sweating like the cow she is. She walked to the passenger's side and then tossed her bags onto the back seat of the car. By the way, for those of you who don't know, Lace is a horrible houseguest. She's demanding and acts as if she's accustomed to having servants. If she ever comes to visit you, hire extra help." She winked at Lace and returned to her story. "After Lace pulled her bleached hair into a bun, she pleaded, "Come on Brooklyn, go to this football game. Please, meet this guy. This time, I assure he'll be fantastic. Just think about it."

I held steadfast to my decision. "You're like kidding me, right? I know you've got this thing about widows without mates, but I don't trust you. Your choices really suck with me."

Anyway, I went to the stupid game. I had no idea Winston was one of the players. That fact, Lace had kept hidden. When the game was over, there was an after party — another fact Lace didn't mention. If I tell you the room was filled with dolls, believe me. I couldn't have been anything special to this guy, I assure you. Well, I was sitting on an ottoman when this incredibly sensual guy squatted beside me. He looked like everything your mother ever warned you about. Six-five. Dark hair. Rugged. Totally charming. I saw him on the field, but up close, I thought I had died and gone to Macy's.

"Let's be honest," I said, sweeping my eyes across his broad shoulders. "I'm not your type at all."

He grinned. "How would you know?"

"Just look around this room. These women look like Barbie dolls. They're flawless."

"Perhaps," he raised a brow, "I don't want flawless."

"You're kidding, right? I mean—who wouldn't want them?"

"I don't want a flawless outer shell. It's what inside that count."

Immediately, I became numb. Nervous in his presence, I turned my head and sipped my soda.

Winston placed his fingers beneath my chin, turned my face, and gazed into my eyes. "Lace told me all about you. I'm sorry about your husband."

"Thank you. What about your wife? I heard you were divorced."

He nodded toward a woman in the company of several men. "She's there."

"That's your ex-wife?" She was a stunning blonde. I couldn't take my eyes off her.

"She was."

"Are you sad about this?"

"No." He expelled a sigh. "She was a gold-digger. I was burned. I learned my lesson."

"Sorry to hear that."

Winston picked up my hand and I stood up. "Please. Let's talk where it's not quite so noisy. I swear I won't try anything funny."

I looked at the drink in his massive hand. "Before we go, would you like another drink?"

He chuckled. "This is ginger ale. I don't drink."

"My — my. Really."

"No. I don't partake of the vine."

With his hand in the small of my back, Winston led me through the crowd and to the balcony. Once he closed the doors, the party sound abated. "Ah, this is wonderful."

"Do you smoke?"

"I'm sorry." He frowned and peered inside the busy room. "I don't smoke. But, if you smoke, I'm sure I can find a cigarette for you." Suddenly he lunged forward.

"No." I placed my hand on his forearm. "I don't smoke. I'm asking if you smoke."

Winston shook his beautiful head. "I afraid not. ...don't smoke. ...don't do drugs.

Guess I'm no fun, huh?"

This gorgeous specimen was standing in the night air, telling me he was no fun. I had goose bumps running up and down my arm. "Pretty soon, you're going to tell me you're a Christian."

Winston winced, and leaned against the railing. "Is that a problem?" He rolled his glass between his palms.

"Well. No. It's just that most successful men don't bother to acknowledge God."

"Brooklyn." He brushed a stray curl from my cheek. "With all that I am, I acknowledged God for my successes. My failures, I blame on myself. I believe that everything in life happens for a reason. It leads you on your life's path. For instance, I can't help but feel you were placed in my life for a specific reason."

Hearing his reasons, I shifted my weight. "For lack of a better word — really?"

Winston nodded, and engaged my eyes. "In my world, most women don't take time to give God his due. What are your thoughts on that?"

Sincerity poured from his lips. My chest was elevating on his every word. Could this be real? Did Lace actually introduce me to a wonderful guy? I looked inside the penthouse. Almost covered by the crowd, I noticed Lace was shaking her royal booty. Outside, with Winston at the helm, the ambience was cool, and mellow. The skyline was majestic — intoxicating.

"Perhaps, I'm out of line." I cleared my throat. "But, I agree with you. Since Wayne died, I've met some weird individuals. I wouldn't leave my dog alone with most of them. You're different, aren't you?"

"Yes. And people frown on me for my beliefs. I'm not a nut and I don't try to shove my religious convictions down a person's throat."

"Most people love the charisma of public figures. How could anyone not believe in you?"

Winston shrugged. "Somehow, we've forgotten what's important in life. First, it's family. If you take care of your family, you'll be doing what God wants you to do. Then, take care of the sick. Feed the homeless…"

"Stop. Are you telling me you have time to do all these things and play pro football?"

"You got me." He chuckled. "I show up as much as possible. However, I pay Matt to keep up with most of my projects. Boys Home, YMCA, Battered Women's Shelter…"

I was struggling to wrap my brain around

what he was saying. "Please. You're too good to be true. Why are you still single?"

"Well. I wanted Crissy. So, I married her. God had other plans."

Brooklyn stopped talking. Her eyes watered. "Guys. I can't go on. This man—this man…" Tears erupted from her soul. "When Winston asked to become a part of his life. I had to say, yes. I had never…"

Shelda stroked Brooklyn's back. "Shh. It's okay. We understand. Don't say anymore."

A box of tissue had started to circulate around the room. An outburst of applause went up. "That is the most romantic love story I have ever heard," Yara added. She wiped tears with the back of her hand. Lace sat in the corner and sulked, jealousy eating her alive. "I could have had him first, but he wasn't my type."

Beth Wedding

CHAPTER TWELVE

After a long night of swapping love stories, the girls finally gave in to fatigue. One by one, they disappeared upstairs to their rooms. Timothy slumped in an armchair, appearing drained. Of course, he had entertained houseguests before, but nothing like the officers from the Cougar Charm dance line.

These women were messy, loud, crass, and nosey. They swapped stories and gave advice like Dear Abby advocates. Finally, Lace had to say goodnight. She picked up her cell on the way upstairs. "Mother is ready to crash," she said softly. Instead of walking up the stairs, she plopped down on the third step. "Guys. I'm too exhausted to walk."

"What'd she say?" Yara asked, raising her weary head from the comfort of the thick carpet.

Shelda was nodding and seemed to be holding on by a thread. "She said there were two egg hawks in the walk."

"Oh." Yara rubbed her eyes. "Really?"

"I slipped upstairs to escape the insanity.

I'm already dressed for bed." Shelda lay prone on the sofa. "I think Lace said, something was broken or something."

"Oh." Yara moaned, nestling her head in the padding of the carpet. "I hate to go upstairs. I'm too exhausted to walk."

"Me too." Shelda replied.

Olivia walked past Lace, dressed in a long satin gown and robe. "Tired, are we? What would Mother Cougar say if you had a performance in the morning?"

"Forget Mother Cougar." Shelda sighed. "We don't have to perform and I'm dead tired."

The front door opened and the three gasped. Hearing footsteps padding down the hallway they turned to each other. "Who is that?" Olivia whispered, crouching behind the doorframe.

Yara raised her tired head from the floor. "I dunno." She yawned. "Whoever he is, he's cute."

Shelda licked her lips and closed her eyes. "Rob me first, please," she said, with slurred words.

The guy was dressed in a light-weight jogging suit.

Obviously, he didn't see the women in

the game room; he went straight up to Lace with an energized trot. "Did you miss me?" He kissed her forehead.

Olivia gawked at Yara. "For a robber, he sure knows his way around the house. I don't think that's a robber at all. I think he's a cookie."

Shelda frowned. "A what?"

"Her cookie. Her playmate. Her stud service," she explained.

"Oh. Oh—." Shelda exclaimed. "He must be going to her room. I guess that's who she called a moment ago."

Olivia looked upstairs. "It must be nice. No batteries required."

Lace yelled from the stairs. "I can hear your conversation. Now, shut up and go to sleep."

* * * * *

The next morning Lace was up with the sun. She had arranged to have Timothy serve breakfast out by the pool. Brooklyn came down stairs and stepped into the morning sunlight. She wriggled up to Lace. "Kiss—Kiss," she said. "How did you sleep?"

Grinning Lace replied, "I slept well, thank you."

"I was sleeping well, too, until I started

hearing voices. It must have been a bad dream. I was so tired."

Lace nearly spilled her juice. "Probably so."

Olivia came dragging out to the pool. "Guys. I swear I've never been this exhausted."

"You just need a bite then you'll feel better," Lace encouraged.

"I need the kinda bite you had last night." Olivia smirked, then folded her brown arms.

Lace sputtered, "I guess you heard noise, too?" Olivia nodded.

"That's why I live alone. Women can be so jealous!"

Brooklyn poured some pineapple juice and sat down. "What's going on?"

Olivia placed her face directly in Lace's face. "Someone had a cookie last night."

Lace smiled. "I said, except in my room." She gawked at Olivia. "You educated butt." Simultaneously she changed the subject. "You pigs are going to work out before we go shopping."

"No. Please. We're too tired."

Lace was adamant. She finished chewing her turkey bacon. "I mean it. I can't keep this body by being lazy. Now, to the gym."

"You are kidding." Yara flopped across a chair. "I need a coffee."

Satin finished her second plate. "We're too full to work out, Lace. Plus we're supposed to be finishing that float."

"Come on, have a heart," Olivia begged, munching her honey dew. "Okay. I'm ready. Let's, go…"

Lace ushered everyone to her the gym. "We can discuss the float later. This is how I keep this gorgeous figure men desire."

"Love that sofa!" Yara smiled. "It's kinda rustic looking."

"Oh, it's strictly for relaxing between sets." Lace pointed to her right. "You get on that treadmill. And you, get on that bicycle. We're going to do a thirty-minute work-out."

Olivia slumped over the treadmill. "Why do hotels need gyms? Save it, Captain. We don't care if we lose our figures, right now."

"Shopping." The women leaped to their feet.

"When?" they said.

"After we work out. Now get to it. A little music will help."

Soon the women were sweating. They chatted and challenged the other's stamina.

Dirty Lace

When Lace reached for the remote and turned off the music, the girls dismounted their equipment. They walked over to the sofa. Each of them fell backward with a sigh.

Satin rolled her neck and shoulders. "If we don't go shopping, we won't get our 70's outfits. Plus, there's this new club I heard about. It's a coffee café. The audience can present their talents. Anyone can perform."

Olivia turned toward Scraps. "Really? I love coffee cafés with poetry. I've been known to do a little something myself. If we go today, I'll show you what I'm really made of."

Brooklyn decided to work out a while longer. As she rode the stationary bike, she became lost in another painting of a bayou. She peddled and gazed at the painting. The others talked, but Brooklyn said nothing. Suddenly, she revved the bike faster and faster until her speed seemed unheard of. Her eyes locked on the painting.

The sudden whirling sound of the bike drew Lace's attention. Brooklyn broke into a sweat and started to moan. Gnashing her teeth, she screamed as if in agony. She stopped and shoved the heavy bike onto the floor. As one stricken blind, Brooklyn made her way to a nearby bathroom.

Lace was troubled and went after her. After thirty minutes of intense sobbing, Brooklyn allowed Lace to enter her space. With her arms wrapped around her friend, Lace brought Brooklyn back to the gym. She sat her down on the sofa.

Yara urged, "Brooklyn, tell us what you're feeling."

Brooklyn started to sob again.

"Let it out," Yara insisted, patting her grieving friend. "You're with friends. Get it off your chest. I'll bet you never properly grieved over your husband. Did you?"

Brooklyn looked up; her eyes were red and swollen. "I'm sorry guys. It's that darn painting. That area looks just like the place they found my husband's body. It's my last memory of him. It's driving me insane."

Brooklyn started to dry her tears. She tried to explain her feelings about his murder. The girls listened. From time to time, they stroked her shoulders to display their concern. "I'm so sorry," Brooklyn bellowed. "I am happy. I know I'm getting married, and to a wonderful man, but…"

Dirty Lace

Lace, Yara, Shelda, Satin, and Olivia all stood in silence. Satin sighed. "Wayne's death will always haunt her. Only time will heal her pain. Now, her life is changing again."

Lace stood up. "I know it's early, but I need a smoke, and a drink."

CHAPTER THIRTEEN

Brooklyn had stolen the morning. All hopes of fun took on overtones of a funeral in progress. The girls tried desperately to appear upbeat about their trip into town. They climbed into Lace's SUV, expecting a day of shopping and fun. Because Cougar County was so small, they drove to a nearby city to relax and enjoy life.

They had their hair colored and trimmed, their nails filled or polished, and feet pampered and soothed. Recently reduced bodies shimmied into tight new dresses or bell-bottoms. The evening was set. Despite the fact that the morning had been morose, the evening filled with laughter and off-key jokes. Occasional conversation with old school chums turned into the highlight of the day. Discussion of the float took a backseat compared to the enjoyment the girls were having.

Giggling, but hungry, Lace took the girls to her favorite coffee café. "Time to wind down with a great coffee. We'll top it off with flavored

cream." Lace pushed the door open and held it
for her friends. "Now, this coffee shop might not
be the norm, but I love it. This time of day, they
have poetry reading, ballads, and skits in
progress. I find it enthralling."

"Somehow, I didn't take you for the
enthralling type," Brooklyn quipped. She was
almost running to keep up with the group.

Looking back at Brooklyn, Lace replied,
"You butt. What kind of crack was that?"

"Well," Brooklyn admitted, "I could
understand your drinking coffee as a companion
to your cancer sticks, but ballads, and poetry.
I'm really shocked."

Lace searched for a table in the darkness.
She gave Brooklyn a nudge. "Just shut up and
walk."

Inside, the room was dimly lit. Several
round tables encircled a hazily illuminated
wooden stage. When the women saw the
performance, they froze in their tracks.

A young woman stood on the stage. With
animated movements, she poured out her heart.
She paraded dramatically as rhymes flowed
from her lips with candor.

As if in agony, the woman tore at her face
as each word forced itself through the chambers

to her thin lips. With vigorous movements, she mimicked an animal given poison in research, only to die on stage. A hail of approval came from the crowd.

"She can't be for real," Yara whispered.

Shelda replied, "I know, right?"

Lace ushered them to her favorite table near the corner. "This is the best table in the house."

Olivia admitted, "I can get into this sort of thing myself. I love doing poetry on stage. I love dramatic and dark poems."

"You would, Olivia. Anything to be on stage," Satin acknowledged, rubbing her large belly.

"Oh, really?" she defended. "You girls think this is funny. How would you know unless you heard my poetry?"

Lace was horrified. "You wouldn't."

"Watch me," she said, getting up from her seat.

Before a server had taken their orders, Olivia was standing on stage. She studied for a moment then she raised her hand to halt the clapping of the crowd. Motionless, she instructed, "Give me a drumbeat, please. The drumbeat started slow, and continued the same tempo as instructed by Olivia.

Then, as if transfixed, Olivia went to a level the girls had never seen. "The Evolution of the Black Female. I said, The Evolution of the Black Female." The small crowd gave a grunt to urge her on. She spoke strong and clear. Her voice echoed off the dark walls with a resonance given to a gospel preacher. "There was a time when a black woman wore her intelligence like the dress on her back. There was a time when being a lady was the ultimate goal of any woman." She walked toward the right of the stage and addressed the patrons sitting in the front area. "The example a Black woman set before her children was close to flawless." She nodded. "Children had their bath and went to bed at a respectable time. Children ate the food put before them, whether they wanted to eat it or not.

Children were taught to respect adults with a yes ma'am and a no ma'am." The crowd agreed with gentle nods. "No child had privacy in their parent's home." Her eyes grew wide. "They owned nothing their parents could not see, read, or taste." She addressed the left side of the stage. "A child would not tell a black woman, *no*. If so, they would find themselves getting up from the floor in a daze. Now, throughout the stores and malls, children degrade their parents, in great detail. I hate you, they say. Get out of my life, they say."

She hung her head in silence, then looking toward the ceiling she spoke. "There was a time when being called a bitch was a major insult. Now, that insult, is highly esteemed as a badge of honor—a rite of passage, an obtainable goal that must be reached. If you're not a bitch, you're no one.

There was a time when man had to imagine what was beneath a woman's clothing. Now, his eyes have free will to sample the goods before buying the apple. Then, when he bites that apple, he simply tosses it at will. Oh well, if he left a seed. Tough luck, baby. It's yours."

As if parting waters with her hands she continued to speak. "There was a time when using correct English meant you had enough pride to speak it. Now, correct English is frowned upon. People are told they're boosie, uppity—if they present themselves in an intelligent light."

She studied a moment. "My grandmamma and your grandmamma took pride in correct English. Distinct syllables meant exactly what they said. There was a time, when attending worship, service was not debatable. There was a time, when a woman appeared to walk behind her man, but actually, without her, he was unable to stand. The Evolution of the Black Woman." With that being said, Olivia bowed her head, then stepped down from the stage.

Lace applauded with a slow methodical clap, typical of the coffee shop environment. As Olivia neared the table, Lace admitted. "I didn't know you had it in you. Now, what the heck were you babbling about?"

"I didn't think you'd understand. That one was for my Sistas," she said, bowing before the table.

Lace grinned and sipped her coffee. "If you're trying to save the planet, I'd say you're on the right track. Put me down for a healthy donation. I'm already going green."

"Oh, shut up you," Olivia teased, fixing her skirt beneath her.

"It's my turn," Yara announced, leaping from her chair. Lace caught her by the arm. "Where do you think you're going?"

Yara stared into Lace's eyes. "I have a statement to make, too," she chided.

Lace let go of her arm. "Oh, what the, hell. Go ahead. Let's hear what you have to say. Brooklyn, are you next?"

Brooklyn threw her hand over her face in defense, then parted her fingers. "You are kidding, right?"

Yara approached the stage. She grasped the microphone in her small hands. Looking upon the audience, she started. "You might feel-ever so good. Your mind, buoyant like pieces of driftwood. Floating along in radiance and peace. Your troubles melt at your feet. Insubstantial, life might be. In your quest to break loose, be free. Troubles melt like night turned day. And calls your soul to melt away. Feathery light and weightless glee, you wake to find, reality. Your beam of light has gone away and you must steal another day." Yara bowed. "Thank you ladies and gentlemen. Choose to be, drug free."

Now satisfied, Yara stepped off the stage to a hail of clapping.

Shelda patted her back as she sat back down. "Wow. You are really serious about your job."

Dirty Lace

Lace sat back and gazed at Yara. In her heart, she knew full well where Yara drew her passion.

CHAPTER FOURTEEN

Brooklyn addressed Olivia. "I thought you were going to speak about love affairs — Chase in particular. I heard you guys broke up."

"That is true. We didn't break up because he's Caucasian. So erase those ideas." She lowered her shoulders and sighed. "I'm not completely healed — it was so traumatic. Since then, we've tried to get back together."

Lace nudged Olivia. "I heard you found out some terrible secret."

"That's also true, but I'll only share this part with you guys.

"See, Chase and I had been living together for two years. A stray bullet found its way into my laptop. That's when I found out Chase was into some risky activity." The women gasped. "I know, right? With Chase being a lawyer and all — it's a freakin' shame. All that ability and talent simply washed down the drain. I still see him, occasionally. But, that's not why we really broke up. The man will do anything to get high. Recently, he borrowed some money from some shyster. That's when our lives changed. He owes money outta the butt. Call me an idiot, but I still love him.

One night, we went out. We took a taxi because we had an agreement that if we planned to drink, we wouldn't drive. Inside the club, the music was loud and the lights were dim. Chase got up to use the restroom. When he reached the door, some hulking Hispanic guy approached him. Doing the club scene, it wasn't uncommon to be dressed in black. But, this time, things didn't feel right. There was tension between them. This was not a typical conversation. From the guy's threating stance, he meant to do Chase some bodily harm. There was a heated exchange of words. I have no idea what was said.

Finally, Chase returned to the table. He was white as a sheet, but he wouldn't volunteer any information. "What's up with that clown?" I asked. "Looks like he's got a problem with you."

Sweat poured from Chase's forehead. You would have thought he was facing a firing squad. "Ah, nothing. Just some yahoo, wanting to borrow money."

"I hope you didn't loan him anything. Things are getting a little tight, you know."

"Yeah. I know." He stroked the back of his neck and kept looking over his shoulder. I'd never seen him so nervous.

"Have you talked to the police about those stray bullets that came through our apartment window? The nerve of some people. Why would someone just randomly shoot at our window?"

"I told you, I don't know," he yelled.

"Woah. What's with the yelling? I simply asked you a question."

Chase looked behind him once more. He seemed concerned about the guy in the shadows. I know Chase well. He was bugging-out. "Look. Let's go. I've had enough of this place."

Before I could ask why, Chase stood up, then walked off, and left me standing by the table. Once outside, we hailed a taxi. When one arrived, Chase opened the door. Just as we stepped inside, the world turned in slow motion. Glass shattered all around us—pelting my body with shards of agony."

Glued to Olivia's conversation, the girls reacted physically to the horrifying news.

"Shut up. What happened?" Appearing frightened, Yara placed her mug clumsily on the table.

Lace shook her head and folded her arms. "That's a dangerous life. I'll bet it was another stray bullet."

"You're right." Olivia nodded. "It *was* another stray bullet. Several in fact. And this time, it did some damage." She tugged at the neckline to her blouse. Her display revealed healed gashes, cuts, and nicks. "I could tell these fools meant business. This girl was not ready to punch her time clock, so I made Chase fess up.

That night, I put his feet to the flame. He confessed about his drug addiction. Then, he told me he had cheated a guy out of some money. He didn't want me to know any details." Olivia looked into the eyes of each friend. "Girls. I know Chase is a loser. I can't help the way I feel. He's the man for me. I don't know if I should fight for him, or get completely out of his life."

Moaning, Lace rolled her eyes. "You're better than that, Olivia. Chase is going no place fast. Right now, he has reservations for a suite at the state pen."

Satin had been quiet, but this time she spoke up. "Olivia. Take it from me. Let him go, babe. He needs help. To help him, let him go.

You're his safety net. In the process of trying to save him, you could meet your end. It's not worth it, girl. You're much too important." Reaching out, she squeezed Olivia's hand.

CHAPTER FIFTEEN

After the entertainment at the coffee café the girls were excited and wired. With electrified movements, they strutted down the street. "Where are we going now?' Yara asked.

Lace smiled a devilish grin. "I'm not telling. It's a surprise." She looked at her watch and started to walk faster.

"Hold up!" Satin puffed. "I not in great shape like you guys. There are *two* of us, you know."

Lace pointed. "There." She looked at an apartment building across the street.

"We're going in there?" Olivia asked, catching her breath. "Who lives there?"

Ignoring their questions, Lace marched on. "Never mind, you'll see."

When they got inside the building, they ran for the elevator. Lace pressed the button to the third floor. Tired and breathless, the girls stood still and waited. They had no idea what to expect. After they got off the elevator, they rushed down the hall with Lace looking at her watch. When they reached room 342, Lace stopped and knocked on the door.

The door opened slightly. A mature female voice called, "Cougar Charms, dress center!"

"That sounds like — like, Mother Cougar!" Yara admitted, with a pleasant smile.

The door opened and Mother Cougar stood before them. She was dressed in a chic top and slacks. "Beyond a doubt, she looks totally great." Shelda nodded.

"Will the woman ever age?" Brooklyn asked, looking over the middle-aged black woman.

"Lace you tricked us," Satin wailed, striking Lace on the shoulder.

Mother Cougar did look exceptional. Ten years had not hurt her one bit. Her dark slanted eyes were striking, but strangely sensual. Because she worked out, her caramel colored skin was healthy and toned. Although, she managed her own hair, it was silky thick and shoulder length.

Guys at school had often made remarks about her shapely lips. "Man she's gotta pretty mouth," they'd say, taunting the instructor.

Dirty Lace

Mother Cougar loved to laugh, but at times, she became a mysterious goddess who seemed to float above ground. She hugged the girls one by one and lined them up in her spacious living room. They stood with shoulders erect and feet together. Even Satin got into the act. "Captain Garnett, where is your whistle?" she demanded.

"It's in my gym bag, Mother Cougar."

A horrid grimace contorted her face. She looked Lace in the eyes. "You might be a talented young lady, but can you blow your whistle from your gym bag?"

"No. Mother Cougar. It will never happen again."

She walked casually in front of Olivia. "Olivia Talbert, get that kinky bird's nest you call hair, *up*, and off your shoulders!"

"Yes. Mother Cougar," she said, grooming her dark tresses.

Mother Cougar then looked at Brooklyn with her piercing dark eyes. Sweeping her gaze over her body, she finally gawked at Brooklyn's nails. "Brooklyn Yohn! That is not regulation nail polish. Remove it immediately or I will remove it for you."

"Yes, Ma'am!"

Stepping in front of Shelda, she shook her head. "Shelda Kingsley, or should I say Piggy May Kingsley? You drop those pounds before Thursday."

"But."

"Did you say, butt? That is exactly what you have, and plenty of it. Now drop that butt, by Thursday."

"Yes. Mother Cougar." she replied, averting her eyes.

Looking at Yara, she scoffed. "You look like a whitewashed picket fence. More make-up. They can't see your pea face from the field like that."

"Yes, Sir."

Mother Cougar paced back and forth in front of the girls. Suddenly, she expelled, "At ease, girls."

The girls burst into laughter.

Lace smiled and wiped her glistening forehead. "It's been a long time."

"I even felt a little nervous." Yara shuffled.

Lace scoffed, "You would."

The girls sat down on the sofa. They remarked that the apartment was tastefully decorated, with an oriental flair. After a while of playing catch up, they got down to questions they always wanted to know about Mother Cougar.

Lace thumbed through a magazine resting on the glass coffee table. "Why on earth did your mother name you Princess? Was she smoking something illegal at the time?"

Chuckling, Mother Cougar explained. "I'm named after my grandmother. My mother expected great things for her children, so she named us accordingly. My brother's name is Chancellor. He's now a judge in Bridgeport. My sister's name is Finesse. She's a Customer Service Manager.

Lace grimaced, and crossed her legs. "Yeah, but Princess?"

Yara smiled. "I like her name. Princess Young. You must admit, it does sound regal."

Olivia raised her hand. "I have a question. You don't mind do you?"

"Go ahead Lieutenant. Ask away." She relaxed into a chair, which oddly resembled a throne from the Ming Dynasty era.

"It's kinda personal."

Mother Cougar seemed puzzled. "It's okay. I'll do my best to answer any question."

Brooklyn looked at Shelda. They knew what was coming. Like a bolt from the blue, Olivia asked, "Did you have an affair with Coach Royal?"

"You aren't kidding, are you?" Mother Cougar grinned.

Olivia shook her head. "Nope."

Shelda stated her case. "Like, we were wondering how you two managed to work together. He was like, totally fine and totally sexy."

"Plus, he wasn't married," Olivia said with a twang.

"And, he was totally fine and gorgeous," Yara agreed again.

"And don't forget sexy," Lace added, hoisting her breasts.

"Girls. Girls. Coach Royal and I were friends. We had a working relationship. He had a woman in his life and I had a man in my life. We were both serious about our personal relationships."

"Cougar swear!" they chimed, with pinkie and thumbs extended.

"Cougar swear," she said, displaying their private hand signal. "Even today, we're still the best of buddies. He even stayed over a few times when we got back late from away games."

"And nothing happened?" Olivia asked, shaking her head.

"Nothing ever happened. We are both mature adults, comrades. Sure he's all that, but I was in a relationship at the time. I was only doing a buddy a favor. I'd do it for any staff member."

"But, even I don't understand that one," Lace admitted. "If I were given the opportunity to be with a really cool, totally sexy guy, who is 6 feet and 5 inches, with a personality — that's professional, confident, enthusiastic, and smart, I'd…

"Mmmm," Olivia moaned. "Plus, he looked totally delicious in those sweats. Girl, when Coach Royal came into the gym, I'd forget all my eight count."

Yara spurted. "Once, we almost kissed." She blushed.

"Oh, do tell," they squealed.

Yara went on speaking. "Well, we had just finished a performance, right. The players were ready to come back on the field, right. As we walked past the boys, Coach leaned over and said, "Great job!"

The girls grabbed a pillow from the sofa and started to smack her. "Oh, Yara. Get a life!" Satin blurted.

Satin shifted her weight on the softly padded sofa. "The name, Princess Royal does have a nice ring to it!"

Mother Cougar joked, "…not written in the stars—my friend."

Soon arms and legs were sprawled across the plush sofa. Elegant shoes became a mixed pile on the carpeted floor. Purses were thrown into heaps of scrunched leather with contents spilled. Although, the girls were comfortable and full, they continued to eat the snacks Mother Cougar had prepared.

After two slices of cheesecake from the coffee café, Shelda still found room for more snacks. Brooklyn reminded Shelda she had promised to tell the unpleasant details about Jackson's behavior. "Now, tell us what happened with Jackson after you guys got back together. Were things ever the same?"

"No they weren't the same," Shelda snarled. "I just couldn't forgive him." She scratched her head. "Pretty soon our entire marriage went to pot. His gambling was tearing everything apart. Our credit cards were maxed out. He had borrowed money from all our closest friends. Soon we were dodging people everywhere we went.

Let me tell you what Jackson did the day after Christmas. This stunt was totally unforgivable. He told our daughter that she couldn't ride her bike because it was defective. Actually, he took the chain loose so she couldn't ride it."

Lace interrupted. "Don't tell me he returned it to the store."

"Yes, he did—along with my new microwave and a few other items. I'd have to say he returned about five hundred dollars worth of merchandise that day. That night, he disappeared. I knew he was gambling again, but I just didn't want to believe it. I got Nana to watch Katelyn while I went to look for him."

"Why?" Yara cried. "When he hit rock bottom, he would have come home."

"Yes. But, when he hit rock bottom, he took us with him. Guys. I really didn't mean to stab him. Somehow, I just lost it."

Olivia made a lone silent clap. "Girl, even though you cut his butt, you forgave him too easily."

"I know, but I was working through some anger issues, myself."

Mother Cougar closed a nearby cabinet. "That was some story, Shelda. I'll bet ten years caused all of you to mature."

"Oh, yes," Brooklyn added, "and in ways we never imagined."

Yara rambled in her handbag. "I could tell you guys some things that would make your hair stand on end. You think life dealt you a bad hand? You think the grass has been green on my side of the fence? If anyone has matured over this ten year period, I would have to say it was me."

Shelda raked crumbs from her skirt. "Yeah, I heard you got into some trouble or something."

Yara shot back, "Wrong. Trouble found me. If not for trouble, I would not have met the love of my life."

"Terrance, right?" Olivia said with an evil grin.

Yara took a pillow and swatted at Olivia. "No. And you know better. How could you be evil enough to say such a thing?"

Brooklyn shrugged. "What really happened? I've heard some pretty wild stories."

"Tell us about it," Satin urged. "Didn't you, like pull a guy from a car wreck or something?"

Staring off into space Yara's thoughts seemed far away. "I hate to think about it." She frowned. "The car was upside down. One of the wheels was still spinning when I pulled my car over. There was smoke and fire pouring from the vehicle. At first, I didn't see anyone. The wreckage was so awful; I felt the impact had thrown him clear. Unfortunately, a man was pinned beneath the car. He appeared helpless. Blood was everywhere."

Yara touched her chest. "I'm not going to tell you I was brave. I wasn't thinking at all. I simply rushed toward the flames. The man moved his head; I knew he was alive. There was moaning as if he was in tremendous pain, and he was turning pale." Yara closed her eyes as if entranced.

"Can you hear me?" I called. "Try to open your eyes. I'm going to see if I can get you out of here before the car explodes."

He groaned, but didn't respond. Girls, he looked like an angel. My heart went out to him. Suddenly, his body started shivering. Because he had lost a lot of blood, I knew he was going into shock. At the risk of being sued, I pulled him from the wreckage. Both legs were broken. They moved independent of his body as I drag him from the ditch, to safety. As soon as I had him free, the car exploded.

The guy opened his eyes. They were the richest green I'd ever seen. I was feeling like a shero, and my heart raced. The paramedics said I did an excellent job. For some reason, I couldn't leave him. I stayed at the hospital until his family arrived. That's when I learned all about this marvelous man.

His name was Houston Golson. He was thirty-three, and new in town. He'd moved into the Briars Apartments. The wreck took place only yards from his residence. Golson's Construction was going to build the new hospital on the west side of town. Guardians of Mercy was going to be one of the largest hospitals in the area. Now, Houston was at someone else's mercy.

Both legs were broken as well as his left arm. He needed someone. I couldn't just walk away. Mrs. Golson, his mother, was a jewel. Each day, we both sat by Houston's side. Then one evening, Houston woke up, and I was there."

Dirty Lace

"What's your name," he asked, biting his chapped lips.

Walking out of the shadows, I grasped the railing around his bed. "I'm Yara Dobson."

He closed his eyes. "Are you my nurse?"

"No. I pulled you from the wreckage. I just couldn't leave you."

Houston turned his face from mine. "I owe you my life."

I felt as if I had the upper hand and stuck to Houston like glue. Sure, it was unfair, but this way, I could win this precious guy. I know I took advantage of his helpless situation, fed him, washed his hair, and cared for his every need. Then one day, Houston was able to walk. Together, we walked out of that hospital and into a new life. I wouldn't take anything for Houston. Call it divine intervention, or call it whatever you like. Houston is the man I prayed for."

Satin spoke, "I never expected anything like that from you."

"And, I guess you became pregnant by taking a purity pill," she defended.

The girls squealed. "What about that other guy, Joshua?" Brooklyn questioned. "I was sure you two had a future together. What ever happened to him?"

"Oh, Joshua." Her nose twitched. "I'll tell you about him, later. Let me finish telling you about this guy. Houston remained a trooper. He was walking on crutches when suddenly this witch flew into town. I met her down on his worksite. Pretty brunette. She announced to me that she was Houston's girl. I was afraid Jenna was a threat to our happiness. The woman was gorgeous. True to her character, Jenna was about to make the first move to win Houston back. That was something I was not about to let happen."

Olivia squealed. "O. M. G. You hid this juicy stuff from us? Was there a physical fight?"

Shelda shook her head. "I never took Yara for a fighter."

Lace shrugged. "Why don't you witches just lay off. Are you guys still seeing each other?"

Yara swooned. "No Lace. He's all yours," she kidded. "I was about to say we're engaged."

Olivia crowed, "You're kidding. What happened to Jenna?"

"I'll tell you about it, later."

* * * * *

Mother Cougar started to clean up her apartment. "I'm sorry, girls, but I have an appointment this afternoon."

"Who's the lucky guy?" they asked.

"Who said it was a guy?" Mother Cougar frowned. "If you must know, I have a teleconference scheduled this evening. I'm going to sit down with my agent and publisher. We're discussing my new book."

"What? Congratulations," they chimed. "We didn't know you were a writer."

Blushing, Mother Cougar held her glowing cheeks. "Girls. Really, it's no big deal. It's just a hobby. After I retired I was able to dedicate my time to writing."

Brooklyn smiled. "Will the book be released soon?"

She shrugged. "Hopefully, I'll have the manuscript cleaned-up and ready for the last read. Right now, I'm still making small revisions."

Olivia bit down on a cracker and chewed. "Tell us about it. What's the title?"

"Girls. I'm running out of time right now, but I will tell you this." She perched herself back upon her throne. "It's a story about seven friends who came together for a class reunion.

After ten years, their lives had changed drastically. They shared their triumphs and their heartaches."

Yara interrupted. "Sounds like us, guys. We've been sharing stories and giving advice, huh?"

Lace grew peeved. "Will you hush? I can't hear."

Mother Cougar looked at Lace then shook her head. "Lace, you're still rude as hell."

"Thanks. I try hard. Now, tell us about this book thing."

"Just a moment." She stood up and walked to her study. Shortly, she returned holding a single sheet of paper. "The title is Milkweed. Perhaps, this will tell you more."

Pushing her glasses on her nose, she then started to read. "Like the silken bundles of the delicate milkweed, together they were strong. However, time had other plans for these windswept seedlings. Life's scattering produced seven undisciplined wild flowers. A ten year high school reunion brings this unlikely bouquet together. While purging their pain, they expose a friendly imposter who has buried her deceitful roots among them."

Shelda jumped in. "The imposter—she's sleeping with one of their husbands, right?"

Mother Cougar smiled. "I'm not telling anymore than that. If I tell you too much, you might not read the book."

Shaking her head in denial Olivia confessed, "That sounds really familiar and really weird."

"Yeah," Brooklyn admitted. "Spooky."

"I'm impressed," Lace added. "Sounds like an interesting read."

Satin's eyes bulged. "Guys! That book sounds like it's written about us."

"I assure you—it isn't." Mother Cougar laughed. "I know nothing about any of you. I've kept in touch with Kayleigh because she lives here. And, Lace lives such a private life that no one ever sees her. So, there. Anything written in is this book is purely coincidental, so don't go running to your lawyers."

Brooklyn drummed her delicate fingers on the table. "Well, I can't wait to read it. And, even if it does sound like us, so what? Our experiences could help someone else."

"Yeah," Yara injected. "We all go through stuff that causes us to grow as human beings."

Lace interrupted. "Okay. Time to go. We've kept her long enough." She walked over to Mother Cougar. "Smooches. I'll keep in touch, okay."

Mother Cougar shook her head. "Lace, I haven't heard from you, or even seen you, since graduation. Do you still live in that little cottage on the Sayer's Estate? Lace borrowed a sheepish expression and didn't bother to answer. "Keep in touch."

Satin hoisted herself from the sofa. She held on to Lace's shoulder to steady herself. "Shame on you, Lace. You should keep in touch with Mother Cougar."

CHAPTER SIXTEEN

Lace opened the doors to her SUV. "Guys, we really need to work on that float. We're going by the hardware store to pick up a few items. We've got to finish. We'd better get our tails in high gear."

Olivia crawled inside the new vehicle. "It was good to see Mother — I mean, Princess Cougar."

Yara agreed. "That was a pleasant surprise. I can't wait to read her new book. Thanks Lace."

When Lace pulled up to the hardware store, they were surprised to see Kayleigh, pushing a shopping cart on the parking lot. She had two children inside the basket and the eldest child walked beside her.

Satin pointed. "There's Kayleigh. Catch her before she gets in her car."

"Not much of a car." Lace commented. "I've seen BBQ cooked in better looking barrels than that." Lace pulled up beside Kayleigh's car and they all got out.

With all the hugging and squealing, Kayleigh appeared overwhelmed. Her mousy brown hair was thin and scraggly. Although her lashes were long, they were hidden by the moon shape of her sunken eyelids. Her sallow complexion revealed years of worry. A broad smile exposed discolored and chipped teeth.

Kayleigh had a deep southern drawl. As she spoke, she'd drag out each syllable, taking almost forever to finish a sentence. "God done blessed me with three boys," she said. "It's good to see you guys. What are ya'll doing out here?"

"We're working on the float for Saturday," Brooklyn said, shielding the sun from her eyes. "Why don't you join us?"

Kayleigh bit her fist. "I wish I could, but I can't. I'd have to get a sitter and then, take off from work. I have to work on Saturdays."

Yara patted her on the back. "That's a shame. We really miss you."

"Thanks," Kayleigh replied, placing a small bag of supplies in the car. "I miss being there. Believe me; these Little Bucks keep me busy." Her smile broke into an awkward silence.

"Well, I'd better go. I've got to cook supper before I leave for work."

"You're awfully busy," Satin observed.

"I work two jobs. It's kinda hard with Little Buck having autism. It's really hard to get a sitter. Buck can be difficult at times. People don't seem to understand." Kayleigh shook her head. "They think all Little Buck needs is a good spanking, when he actually needs more than that. I kinda stay 'round the house on off days."

Satin was concerned. "When was the last time you went out?"

"It was 'round Christmas, I think."

Olivia shuddered. "Dang. You're almost a prisoner."

"It's okay. I don't mind none. These here boys are my life."

"Are you seeing anyone?" Shelda asked.

"Nah. I ain't got no time for relationships. Buck keeps running in and out of my life. Most men just stay away."

"What time do you go to work?" Yara inquired.

"About seven. It's only a part time job."

Yara had a great idea. "Why don't we take you and the boys out to eat? That way, we could all visit."

Kayleigh stroked her sons' heads and looked into their brown eyes. "I don't wanna be no imposition. Little Buck is quite a handful."

Olivia folded her arms. "There are seven of us all together. I'm sure we can manage. Come on girlfriend, follow us to Ranchland Steakhouse."

"I'd love a good steak." She licked her dry lips. "I git pretty tired of my own cooking."

When they reached Ranchland Steakhouse, everyone was excited. They almost had the restaurant to themselves. Kayleigh's boys were well behaved. Little Buck behaved as well as expected. At any rate, the girls were able to catch up with years of absence.

Kayleigh relaxed and enjoyed her meal. "Yep. That Buck was something else. He hardly comes 'round anymore. I'm pretty much ashamed of him anyways. I don't want the boys to see him when he's high and usually, he's high."

Satin stuffed her baked potato with sour cream. "Why didn't you leave him sooner?"

Kayleigh bit her bottom lip. "When we started out, Buck was a decent person. I think my life got screwed-up the day I was born. As a child, life at home wasn't very good. My daddy drank, and constantly beat my mama. Every weekend was a livin' nightmare.

Even at school, my mind was wrapped around my mama's safety, as well as my own. I was the only girl in my house, so I was responsible for my younger brothers. As my mama's right arm, my job was unendin'. Mama worked at a restaurant on the weekends. She earned very little in tips.

Dad drank heavily. In his drunken stupor, he'd forget he was married. One night, he called us from our beds, lined us up in the kitchen then pointed his gun to our heads. He had my mother kneel execution style while he played Russian roulette with her life. He told us we was next.

I feared for my life, most of the time. I had no doubt that killin' one of his children would come easy for him. When I got older, that fear grew more intense. Mother warned us, that what happens in our house stayed in our house. We didn't breathe a word 'bout the excessive abuse.

I hated the weekend and had to get away. Being a Charm was an outlet. I loved you guys, and you guys loved me back. I felt like I was somebody special in my cute little uniform, and all. Dad loved football and often he attended the games. He didn't mind me being in the dance line. Although he was drunk, he would stand on the sidelines and give me fake encouragement. "Go, Baby Girl!" He would say. "That's my Girl!"

As I blossomed into a young woman, I could feel Dad's grip closing in around me. I knew it wouldn't be long before he would beat me down for good. I grew tired of hidin' the whelts and the bruises. At night, I'd dream. No matter how hard I tried to control my dreams, I always dreamed of killin' him. I had planned the perfect murder in my mind. I didn't want to go to jail. So, I found another way out.

About that time, I met Buck. And, takin' him at face value, I married him and moved away. I know everybody thought I got married 'cause I was pregnant, but I didn't care. I was a bona fide virgin when I married Buck.

As irony would have it, I became the one who was abused. The abuse didn't start right away. It started when Buck started cheatin' on me. He gave me sexually transmitted diseases that he didn't bother to explain. Like my father, Buck would slam plates against the wall to start an argument. And, like my father, the beatin' was linked to alcohol and drugs.

Each day, Buck warned me not to leave the house. When his friends came over for a drink, they'd turn away whenever Buck would strike me, or snatch out a patch of my hair.

Although, there was no food in the house, Buck wouldn't come home for days. I'd look out the window for hours. My transportation to work depended on him. As a result, I lost many jobs.

Buck came home one night. I was in my first pregnancy. He was drunk. He took off his clothes and told me to take off mine. When I refused, he kicked my belly sideways, then started to stomp me. Oh, the pain was bad. Then, I felt a gush. Even at eight months, I knew the baby was on the way. Here I was, naked, and crawling around on the cold floor. Buck knelt beside me. "Is you fixin' to push out that rug rat?"

I was cryin' so hard, I couldn't answer. Then he asked me again. "I said, is you fixin' to have that freak. Whatever it is, it ain't mine."

Buck was so busy getting a beer he didn't notice when I drag myself to the bedroom. By the time I reached under the bed, Buck stepped on my wrist. That's where he kept his gun. "So, what you think you gonna do with that?"

"Honestly, Buck. I'm hurtin'. I was trying to get in the bed."

He looked behind me. "Look at that mess you done made. You done soiled yourself." He took his foot and kicked me over.

Labor pains was hittin' me somethin' fierce. It weren't time for the baby, but I knew once I lost my water, it wouldn't be long. "Please Buck. Let me call my mama. She can help deliver the baby."

"Ain't you fat as a cow? Animals don't need no help."

Buck put on his clothes and stepped over me." Kayleigh raised a brow. "I lost my baby that night. It was a girl. Oh, she was the prettiest thing you ever did see. I held her in my arms all night. When Buck got home the next day, he tore her from my arms and buried her in the back yard."

She took a swallow of her tea. "After that, I kinda didn't care no more. God gave me these boys, and I thank him for that. They mean a lot to me. One day, Buck got drunk and decided he was going to circumcise our newborn son. Well, that's where I drew the line. When he reached for his huntin' knife, I busted him 'cross the head with a kitchen brick."

Yara almost lost her food, while Olivia sat with mouth agape. Dare they say anything?

He was a'skeetin' blood, but I didn't care. I got my son and left. I had been checkin' on a shelter for women that's been beat up. They welcomed me with open arms. Other women were there. They helped me with my child. Finally, I got a little job and struck out on my own. Been working two jobs since.

In counseling, I realized just how vile Buck was. I tried to start my life over, but Buck found me and forced sex. When I refused his invitation, he'd kick in my door and snatch me inside the car. One time, my baby was asleep in the bed when he took me.

He said he only wanted to talk, this time. I knew better. I jumped from his movin' truck before I knew it. I had to get back to my children, but not before Buck put his brand on me. Caught me right here with that ring of his." Kayleigh pointed to the edge of her graying hairline. There, the skin had been torn away. It was obvious she had no medical attention.

"I got pregnant with my last boy when Buck went to rehab. He promised me he would deal with both his addictions. He stayed sober for almost three months. Then Peter was born. I already had Ezra. Shortly after that, Little Buck's conception was a forcible rape. Buck had started back drinkin' and havin' affairs. We were in the process of getting' a divorce when he took advantage of me in front of my boys.

Finally, I was successful at leavin' Buck. I don't care if he never sees the boys. By the time I started my new life, I was scared, mentally, and physically. I wouldn't know how to love a man. I wanted God to give me a man who would love me and treat me accordingly."

Yara held her hand to her mouth. "Oh, my God, Kayleigh. We never knew." Tears ran down Yara's face and she reached for a napkin.

Satin, Brooklyn, Shelda, and Olivia were shedding tears from the moment Kayleigh started talking. Because Yara was a counselor, she was able to hold herself together longer than the others were. Lace simply shook her head.

CHAPTER SEVENTEEN

On their way home, Lace chattered on. "And did you see her teeth. Oh, my God. How much does it cost to see a dentist?"

"Stop it Lace." Shelda demanded.

Lace ignored Shelda's plea. "And that hair of hers. What is that? I've seen hay with more body. I'll pay for her to go to the beauty shop."

Olivia closed her eyes and inhaled. "Please, Lace."

Lace prattled on. "I'm sorry guys, but Kayleigh is nothing but poor white trash."

"What? Oh, no you didn't." Olivia's anger was evident.

"As far as I'm concerned," Brooklyn said defensively, "we're all poor white trash."

Lace frowned. "Your heritage is Asian and Olivia's parents are Black. What *are* you talking about?"

"No." Satin shook her finger. "We got out of Cougar County. Kayleigh didn't."

Lace babbled on. "Did you see those seedy kids? I mean, how much is a bottle of detergent? Yuck."

"That's enough Lace," Shelda said, irritation coating her words. "You're no better than she is."

Lace turned down the street that led to her lovely mansion. "Well, she needs to get a decent paying job."

Satin pursed her lips. "She works at Sayers Electronics. She's a janitor."

Lace's eyes sparked fire. "What do you mean, she works at Sayers?"

Olivia nipped at Lace. "…just what she said. She works at Sayers Electronics. I heard she started working there when she divorced Buck. The benefits really suck. Her child needs doctor's care almost twenty-four seven."

"I'll bet her living conditions are terrible." Shelda moaned.

"Yeah, they are," Satin informed. "She lives in the old project building we lived in long ago. I heard they were going to tear it down in a few months."

"Poor Kayleigh," Olivia added. "Where will she go?"

Knowing she owned Kayleigh's apartment complex, Lace became quiet. She had signed the papers to tear the building down months ago. Where Kayleigh's family laid their heads was not her concern. Was it?

Lace pulled up in the driveway and turned off the car. "Come on guys. It isn't that bad. Kayleigh will be fine. She'll find some other dump to live in." Lace smiled sweetly. "Let's change into some comfortable clothes and get busy."

Dirty Lace

Shortly afterwards, the girls used their staple guns, hot glue guns, and mounds of tape to complete the float. Satin had the job of handing out flowers as the girls busily attached them. After the float was completed, the girls admired their handy work. The float was awesome. There were poppies of orange, yellow, green, red, and baby blue. Brooklyn spent time gluing large leaves where there were open spaces. "Did anyone make the sign?" she asked, standing on a stepladder.

"I'm working on it now," Shelda said, fanning the scents of the pungent markers. Finally, the float was finished. Six females headed for the showers. This would be their last evening together. After the parade, they would all go home.

As they reclined in the media room Yara reminisced. "I hate to go home tomorrow. I've had a blast!"

"Me too," Satin admitted, licking ice cream from her spoon. "Just wait until I tell Davis all about this."

Brooklyn crooned, "Yes, sir. This has been wonderful, Lace, but I can't help but to worry about Kayleigh." She shuddered. "Wonder what we could do to help her. I'd like to have a charity benefit to help her out. If I had the money, I would just give it to her."

"Did you see how she attacked that steak," Yara said. "The poor thing hasn't felt special in years. I'm glad we could take her out."

Lace sat on her favorite chair. "Hey. She's not in bad shape. She's just a lazy slob, I tell you."

Olivia was growing furious. "Lace! How could you look at her and not feel anything."

Shelda munched some popcorn. "I'm wondering the same thing myself, Lace. What's up with you?"

"She just wants our pity. Surely, you're not taken in by that—it's just an act." Lace mimicked Kayleigh. "…and my po li'l old husband beats me e'ry day. Shut up. Enough already."

The girl gasped. "Lace!"

Brooklyn reached for a fashion magazine. "Lace, you're being unrealistic. Leave Kayleigh alone. She's our blood sister."

Lace twirled her finger in the air. "*Your* blood sister."

Thumbing through the magazine Brooklyn confessed. "We're supposed to help each other. You know—that all for one, and one for all crap." She dropped the magazine on the floor. As she reached down to pick it up, she noticed the mailing label. She focused on the name: Lace Garnett, 1616 Garnett Lane. "Lace, I'm puzzled. This magazine has your name on it."

"And so?"

"This address is 1616 Garnet Lane. Something is screwy here."

Yara jerked her head toward Lace. "Lace, how did you do that? You told us you rented this place."

Lace folded her arms. "I never said I rented this place. You *assumed* I rented this place."

Olivia gave Lace a sidelong glance. "This house doesn't belong to you—or does it?"

The girls rose from the comfort of their padded chairs. They looked at each other with amazement. Satin growled. "This is the Sayers Estate. You've got some things to explain."

Standing to her feet, Lace summoned Timothy. He rushed toward the door. Obviously, he'd overheard the caterwauling, and turned on his heels. "Come back here, Timothy."

Timothy waved his hand briskly and stood his ground. "I told you this would *not* be easy. Now, you have hurt feelings to mend."

Lace shrugged and lowered her lids. "It's no big deal. So, I lied." She addressed the angry women. "I only lied so I could fit in with you guys. Now, I wish I hadn't bothered."

"No, she didn't," Olivia crowed, leaping to her feet. "Please hold me back."

Shelda placed her popcorn bowl aside. She narrowed her eyes. "How could you? After all we've been through."

Satin's breathing increased. "So, you flew us out here to rub our noses in your good fortune. Are you kidding me? You — were never poor? I shared my last with you."

Olivia closed in on Lace with a menacing stare. "How many times did you eat at my house, Lace? You stuck your feet under my table and ate whatever my mother prepared."

Yara tightened her fist. "…and, my parents as well! We all shared. That's what *real* friends do."

Tears stood in Shelda's eyes. Her stance was rigid with anger. "My mother gave *you* the dress I was going to wear to the prom. We thought you lived in the cottage next door. We thought Timothy was your father. Are you telling me you could have bought every girl at the prom a dress? How could you be so insensitive?"

Yara gnashed her teeth, and shook her head as if in denial. "And poor Kayleigh. You berated her as if she was trailer trash. Kayleigh was not dumb in school. As a matter of fact, she tutored your dumb ass in algebra."

"Yeah." Olivia poked Lace in the chest. "Kayleigh was the one who always gave gifts to everyone. She baked cookies. She made baskets filled with treats. You ate her snacks didn't you?"

Shelda stroked her forehead. "Kayleigh took the rap for us when we cut class. She didn't have to do that, Lace." She pleaded, "Listen to me. She did detention—for us...all of us—and she never complained. She jeopardized her college scholarship. For us, Lace Garnett. How can we make that right?"

Brooklyn sat in silence. She tapped her fingers against the sofa, but hadn't spoken.

"Brooklyn," Satin asked, "did you know about this little charade?"

"No." Appearing remorseful, Brooklyn shook her head. "I knew nothing of this. Lace came to visit me. Until now, I never visited her."

Yara stormed across the room. When she returned, she stood in front of Lace. "I didn't want to say anything, but Kayleigh is still wearing the Charm ring Mother Cougar bought us—ten years ago. Didn't you see it? It was old and tarnished…no longer gold plated. Our bond meant something to her."

With lips parted, Lace stood speechless. How could her friends turn on her like that? "I can't believe what I'm hearing."

"Well," Olivia yelled, "hear this, Miss Snooty. I'm outta here. I'm glad I drove my car."

Satin waddled to her feet. "Really, Lace. I'm like, so outta here. You're not even close to being the Lace we knew."

Lace stammered. "B, but, Scraps."

"Don't Scraps me. You're a heartless heifer." Satin made her way toward the stairs.

Brooklyn walked past Lace. Lace reached out to her. "Brook."

"Don't touch me." She narrowed her eyes and peeled Lace's fingers from her shoulder. "D, don't touch me."

Dirty Lace

Shelda grimaced, jerked her head, and walked upstairs.

Timothy called to the angry women. "Ladies, please. She's just misguided. She meant no harm."

Seeing her friends walk out of her life, Lace threw herself on her sofa. "I can't believe this. All I've done for them and they just walk out and leave me with this mess. The parade is tomorrow. What am I going to do?"

Yara sat beside Lace. "Sweetie. You need help. You've lived a lie for so long — what did you expect. The Mutt Pack was built on sacrifice and friendship. When one of us was in trouble, we all felt it. Remember the time we threw you a birthday party. You told us Timothy couldn't afford one. Lace, we stole everything we ate from our homes. Together, we made a wonderful meal. We made a wreck of Timothy's kitchen, but the food was great. Guess who arranged it all. It was Kayleigh, honey. Kayleigh." Yara stroked Lace's back. Lace covered her face and shook her head.

"Lacy. I don't know who you've become. I don't know all of your personal secrets and frankly, it doesn't matter to me. Am I angry? Yes. We're all pissed at you. Kayleigh needs you.

She needs all of us. Now, you need to go straight upstairs and apologize to your guests—your friends. These women love you without condition. They loved you when they felt you didn't have a penny. You owe them an apology."

For the first time in years, tears plumped in Lace's eyes. "Yara. Those knuckleheads are all I have. No one else loves me for who I am. They've always cared about me. I've got to make this right." She pounded her fist in her hand, her eyes sparked with fire. "Shortcake. I own Sayers Electronics. That's where Kayleigh works."

Yara's eyes widened. "Tell me you're kidding."

"No." Lace closed her eyes. "First, I'm going to fire Kayleigh."

"Lace!"

"Hear me out. I'm going to fire her and give her a better job. Kayleigh has a heck of a brain. She's always been good with accounting. I'm giving her the job in accounting."

Squealing, Yara hugged her misty friend. "That's so sweet."

"I'm not stopping there. I also own the Greenbrier Apartments."

"Those apartments over on Second Street? The ritzy apartments?"

"Yes. From now own, Kayleigh has a home. She can live there rent free for as long as she wishes."

After kissing Lace on the cheek, Yara rushed up the stairs screaming. "She's back!"

CHAPTER EIGHTEEN

After placing a few phone calls, Kayleigh was standing at Lace's front door. Timothy asked her, and her sons inside. Their virgin eyes were large as saucers as they took in their stately surroundings.

The women rushed downstairs and huddled around Kayleigh. Together, they cried. Kayleigh placed her once battered head on Lace's shoulder.

"Kay." Lace stroked her shoulder tenderly. "Don't cry, sweetie. It's all over. You're protected. I'll see to it that Buck never hits you or your kids again." She raised Kayleigh's chin. "I took the liberty of furnishing your three-bedroom apartment. I hope you don't mind."

This time, Kayleigh lurched forward, and trembling, she fell to her knees. Her sons surrounded her, kneeling—consoling her with gentle caresses. "Don't cry Mama. See, you're finally getting what you deserve. You're a good mama. You always been there fer us."

Dirty Lace

The oldest son gazed into Lace's puzzled eyes. "Ms. Lace here, is gonna give you a job with numbers. You always been good with numbers."

Olivia knelt beside Kayleigh and stroked her sparse hair. "Lace is sending someone to size your children for clothing, Kayleigh." She whispered, "It's your time, sweetie."

Kayleigh got to her feet. "Lord. I can't pay this woman back. I can't pay her. Ya'll don't understand!"

Shelda caught Kay by the arm. "She's not asking for payment, Kay. Just accept it, honey. We love you."

Witnessing Kayleigh's display of grievance, Lace backed up. Finally, she turned and walked toward the sun deck. Yes. She needed a smoke. Never in her life had she ever felt so liberated. Was she having a heart attack? She held her chest and felt her heart racing. With nervous fingers, Lace poured herself a drink. Someone was standing in the doorway, watching her. She glanced up. "Timothy."

Timothy smiled and clapped his hands. "Beautiful performance. I'm proud of you, Lace Garnett. Now, you're like your mother. Your family always helped their fellow man. That's how they became successful. I know it feels strange to you now, but the more you do, the better you'll feel. We were put on this earth to help each other. If you love humankind, you can't sit back and watch them suffer. True happiness comes, when your release what God has given you."

Lace's breath quickened. "I do understand. This feeling—this feeling is… Whew! What a rush!"

"Shh," Timothy assured. "I know how you feel. You're giving the love they gave to you, all those years ago."

"I'll never be the same, Timothy. I swear. Those bats have ruined a perfectly good woman. I promise, I'm helping more people." She sighed. "…to actually see the happiness glistening in their little eyes." Fighting back tears, Lace placed her hands to her trembling lips and swallowed. "I, I can't explain it. It's awesome."

* * * * *

During Saturday's parade, Kayleigh sat on the float with her friends. At Lace's expense, her hair had been conditioned and trimmed—her make-up was impeccable. While Lace watched, Kayleigh was transformed. A large smile replaced years of torment and worry.

Now, Lace could pat herself on the back. "That's what friends are for. Simply amazing."

~THE END~

About the Author

Beth Wedding

Beth Wedding loves God, and she loves writing Christian and Contemporary Romance. Her stories are written to uplift and inspire. Beth gives God the glory for his wonderful inspiration. To learn more about Beth, visit Topaz Publishing Author's page.

http://www.topazpublishingllc.com

www.ingramcontent.com/pod-product-compliance
Lightning Source LLC
Chambersburg PA
CBHW021152020426
42331CB00003B/26